Winewise

At 26, Alice King is the youngest nationally read
wine writer. Sixth in a family of nine children,
she learned about wine at an early age, mimicking
her father's wine-tasting antics (he was
in the wine trade) to amuse her brothers and sisters.

At 18 she went to work for a champagne company in
France, and, after a course in journalism, joined
Decanter, becoming its Deputy Editor after two
years. She is now wine correspondent for the
Daily Mail.

On average, she tastes between 200 and 300 wines
a week – definitely good Winewise training!

ALICE KING

Winewise

or How to be Streetwise about Wine

With illustrations
by Michael Heath

Methuen . London

First published in Great Britain 1987
by Methuen London Ltd
11 New Fetter Lane, London EC4P 4EE
© 1987 Alice King
Illustrations © 1987 Michael Heath

Printed in Great Britain
by Richard Clay Ltd, Bungay, Suffolk

British Library Cataloguing in Publication Data

King, Alice
   Winewise : or how to be streetwise about
   wine.
   1. Wine and wine making
   I. Title
   641.2′2   TP548

ISBN 0-413-16760-7

For Billy Whizz

Contents

Part One Get Winewise!

Introduction   11
1. Bottle Bulge   17
2. Label Fables   23
3. Vintage Guide – Top of the Year   30
4. A Question of Style   33
5. Converting the Grapes   37
6. Grape Expectations – The Fruitful Facts   40
7. Tasting – Enough to Make You Spit!   48
8. What a Corker!   54
9. Glass Farce   60
10. Decadent Decanters   65
11. Cupboard Love   71
12. Bottle Stop   74
13. Auctions – Sometimes a Winewise Bid   85
14. Restaurantwise   89
15. Food and Winewise   93
16. Get Mega-Winewise!   95

Part Two Worldly Winewise

Introduction   99
17. France – The French Connection   100
    Champagne – Bubble Bonanza   100
    The Loire – The Vin Valley of France   107
    Burgundy – Untangle the Confusion   111
    Beaujolais – Not Just the Nouveau Way   117
    Bordeaux – Without Paying the Dough   120
    South-West France – Beefy Reds   128
    The Rhône – Valley of the Giants   132

    Provence – Sun-Drenched Beauties   135
    Alsace – The Spicy Treat   138
18. Portugal – Powerful and Punchy   141
19. Spain – Flamenco Good Value   144
20. England – Not At All British   148
21. Italy – Pasta Partners   151
22. Germany – Life Beyond Liebfraumilch   156
23. Bulgaria – A Chip Off the Old Bloc   160
24. Australia – Down Under Sport   161
25. New Zealand – The Wines are not Extinct   166
26. California – A Sunny State of Mind   168
27. Chile – Hot Stuff!   172
28. A Fortified Tale   173
    Questionwise   178
    Index   184

Part One
Get Winewise!

Introduction

Drink what you want, when you want, where you want – it's called being Winewise!

As children we always did – or at least we tried to. With a father working in the wine trade, we were introduced to wine at a very early age. Being a competitive family by nature – there were nine of us, so we had to be – we quickly became streetwise about most things. Wine was one of the first, fairly high on our list of priorities. In fact, the question has often been posed as to who drank more champagne at the christening, the mother or the baby? Which is not to say my mother doesn't like champagne . . .

Following our christenings (although, coming sixth in the family, I only enjoyed three other than my own) our wine-drinking experiences were confined to Sunday lunch and the very occasional sip on a weekday evening when my parents mistakenly thought we were all tucked up in bed. My mother was convinced that my youngest brother Conrad (who now works in the wine trade) could smell out a bottle from upstairs for, however long he had been in bed, once the cork was drawn he was downstairs as quick as a flash. He was then in the driving seat. If he wasn't given any wine he would make so much noise that at least three or four of the rest of us would descend, meaning far less wine for all. As a result he often enjoyed a secret taste along with my parents and then gloated to the rest in the morning.

In those early days our assessment of any wine was very simple. Either we liked it or we didn't. If we didn't like it we didn't drink it. This is a fundamental Winewise approach. Not that the wine ever went to waste. With less than a second of consideration the glass would have been

whisked away by some more appreciative, generally older, brother or sister.

We were hooked on grapes as little children. They, like wine, were a real treat. Long before we were politically aware of the apartheid situation, there was much licking of lips in the house when every Christmas our aunt in South Africa sent us a whole crate of Cape grapes. These were rationed on a fairly strict basis, but there were those in the family who found their way round this quota system. There was at one time a consensus of opinion that the more grapes you ate the more drunk you would feel. Well, I suppose we were on the right lines!

Normally at the mention of washing up nine children would either vanish into thin air or wage a full-scale battle. But there were always plenty of volunteers to help with dinner parties. The great excitement was that there would be more than one wine to try, and even if we weren't given a taste, we reckoned on at least one person (generally the

long-suffering wife who was talked into driving home) leaving some of their wine on the table.

Towards the end of one of the famous crates of Cape grapes, a magnificent bunch was selected to grace the cheese board. There were many little helpers in the kitchen and dining room that night. When my mother at last came out to collect the cheese board there was now a stem with two mouldy grapes attached where once had been a large bunch of ripe black ones. How could all nine of us have known that the 'few' we had each taken would result in virtual destruction of the bunch? After all we weren't clairvoyant, just opportunists.

Sunday lunch the next day was a sad affair. None of us got so much as a sniff of the wine my parents drank. As it was January, next Christmas and the prospect of more grapes seemed a long way off!

Having a father who was a wine merchant had many advantages. Projects at school, even as early as infant school, took on a vinous flavour. With a steady supply of brightly coloured labels, we were able to produce out-of-the-ordinary projects, always very different from the normal 'My Dog' or 'My Cat' which we thought very boring. This was partly because we didn't have any pets (eight brothers and sisters were enough) and partly because we had already sussed that, for reasons unknown to us, wine was regarded with mystique. We even exploited this by trading labels for the dubious delights of bubblegum or comics.

When I was eight we spent our first summer holiday abroad in a Bordeaux château. One day during the holiday we were invited to lunch at a château in Cognac. A fairly brave gesture for the owners, who had not had the pleasure of meeting the mad English family with nine children. We all had menus with our names on, and this château had even more 'slaves' (our naïve word for the domestic staff) than the one we were staying at (we were amazed that people had real live servants). We were all served a 1920s champagne, followed by a white I don't recollect and half a glass of Château Montrose 1893. Having been taught to taste a wine and pronounce on it we all very seriously tasted

the wine. Knowing better than to spit it out on the floor we delighted in swallowing it. The owner, obviously amused (or outraged, but whatever, incredibly generous), asked us what we thought of the wine. Dominic, the next brother up from me, was nominated as spokesman. It was unfortunate that at that time the boys had an expression, 'two out of ten for trying', which they answered to most questions. This was muttered among giggles around the table. Dominic, however, considered his reply. Beckoning to one of the 'slaves' he said in his best nine-year-old French, *'Encore une bouteille, s'il vous plaît'*.

The owners thought this hysterical. My parents were less impressed, but were perhaps mollified by the appearance of another bottle. In retrospect, I think my brother was definitely Winewise. We knew it was a good wine, but really had no concept of the hundreds of pounds' worth of wine, even then, we were drinking – but we liked it. It was a nice day, but I do recall being sent off to play when the old cognac made its appearance.

But back to the present day. People get really worried that they don't know enough about wine. But at the end of the day, however much you know, the questions are still the same: do you like it, and would you buy it? This book sets out to tell you some of the tricks of the trade, how to get the most out of a bottle, what to look for and where to find the best value for money. It is not in any way supposed to be the last word, but rather a light-hearted guide to the good value wines available and an insight into the up-and-coming areas. Being Winewise doesn't mean you have to read every wine book in sight; it simply means you know what to look for and how to avoid spending hard-earned money on disappointing wines.

The most enjoyable aspect of becoming Winewise is that you simply have to keep experimenting . . . Cheers! *'Encore une bouteille s'il vous plaît!'*

Chapter 1

Bottle Bulge

Do you feel inadequate when confronted by hundreds of bottles in a wine shop or supermarket? Lots of people do, so don't panic — read on!

There's an easy way of telling roughly what's in the bottle, at least as far as European wines are concerned. Many regions have their own distinctively shaped bottle. So if it's a French wine you're unlikely to get confused between Bordeaux, Burgundy and Alsace provided you remember the shape of their bottles. If you have an idea of the style of wine you are looking for, this can be an enormous help.

The Bordeaux Bottle

This is an upright member of society. It has high, straight sides and shoulders (the bulges below the neck) that curve inwards sharply to the neck. The latest version has the word 'Bordeaux' embossed in the glass just below the shoulder. This helps! It is one of the most popular bottle shapes around and it is also used for wines in the south-west of France (not that far geographically from Bordeaux anyway) like Bergerac, Cahors, Corbières, Buzet, Minervois and Fitou. In addition it's used in Italy, Spain, Portugal, California, Australia, Bulgaria and many other countries. Generally red wine is put in this bottle, although it is occasionally used for white wines.

The Burgundy Bottle

This has a dumpier bottom than the Bordeaux bottle, with gently sloping, slouching shoulders — the sort that fit comfortably into an off-the-shoulder ball gown. It's rather like a cylinder with a cone sitting on top of it. Whilst it's most famous for Burgundy (both red and white), it is also used for wines from Beaujolais, the Rhône, the Loire, Spain, Australia and California. When found in non-European countries it is generally used for classic European grape varieties such as Pinot Noir, Sauvignon and Chardonnay.

The German Bottle

An elegant, tall, thin, fluted shape. Rather like a thinner version of the Burgundy bottle. It is used for most German wines, either in green or brown glass, depending on whereabouts the wine is made. Generally a green bottle indicates that it has come from the Mosel, and brown from the Rhine. The German flute is also occasionally used in California and Australia, often when a German grape variety is used or the wine is very sweet. English wine and German lookalikes and tastealikes like Yugoslavian Laski Riesling can be found in these bottles.

The Alsace Bottle

This is very similar to the German flute, but it is slightly taller. It is used only in Alsace.

The Champagne Bottle

This is rather like a Burgundy bottle except that, as it has to contain high pressures, it is made of thicker, dark green glass. (A few very expensive champagnes are bottled in clear glass.) All the Champagne clones (like Blanquette de Limoux, Lambrusco, Saumur, Cava etc.) are sold in the same shape bottle.

Other Bottles

There are a few regional oddballs (or odd bottles!). There's the *bocksbeutel*, the flat, dumpy shape made famous by the Portuguese Mateus Rosé. This is also used for the light, slightly sparkling white Portuguese Vinho Verde and some German Trocken (dry) wines. Various-sized dumpy bottles are used for many different wines, including Cotes-du-Rhône, Frascati and Australian Liqueur Muscat. Skittle-shaped *pichet* bottles are popular in Provence and other areas in the south of France, especially for rosés.

Bottle sizes vary and you should be aware that some bottles are deceptive to the eye. Look for the size, which should be on the label. Most commonly found now are 70 and 75 centi-litres (cl). Many table wines use the former and, with the 7 per cent difference in content, it is worth checking when comparing prices. Most supermarket own-label wines are 70 cl but pioneers Sainsbury's have taken the Winewise lead by introducing the bigger 75 cl bottles.

1.5-litre bottles, or magnums, are not always cheaper than the equivalent two bottles, especially with more expensive finer wines where a supplement is paid because of the extra costs of manufacturing and handling the larger bottle. With less expensive everyday wines, big bottles may be cheaper but again, if you're Winewise you'll check the price and bottle size. Many people are caught out because, as some merchants have realised, they automatically assume the bigger the bottle the better the value.

Half-bottles are often overlooked by merchants but are a great idea if you want to try several wines. As with the magnums, rather than being exactly half the bottle price, they can be marginally more because of the extra price of the bottle. As well as their convenience (especially for solo drinking), wine actually matures more quickly in half-bottles so they can be a way of tasting a mature wine sooner. Generally, if you have a bottle and a half-bottle of the same vintage, the half-bottle will taste more mature. But as it reaches its peak sooner, it's best to lay down bottles for long-term keeping.

There's nothing wrong with plastic bottles, especially if the wine is cheap and cheerful and going to be consumed soon after purchase, and they make shopping, picnics and bike rides less hard work because they're so light.

Of course, you don't have to buy wines in bottles. I mean, it's so old-fashioned (yawn!). With the advent of the metal tin which has been specially treated so that it does not chemically react with the wine, you can now buy wine as well as baked beans in tins. The slimline 25 cl cans around at the moment have helpful ring-pull tops and are handy if you only want a glass, for picnics or when you've lost the corkscrew. It's best to drink soon after purchasing and don't expect them to be good value when compared to the equivalent bottle.

Tetrapacks or tetrabrics seem to have caught on more than cans, and for those of you wondering what on earth a tetrabric is, it's more commonly used for orange juice. Most tetrabrics contain a lot more than you think, usually one litre, although if you stand one next to a litre bottle most people would automatically expect the bottle to contain more wine. Because the cost of packaging isn't prohibitive, they are good value and the majority of the big supermarket chains now sell decent table wine in tetrabrics. Again, the best idea is to drink them straight after purchase. Their main disadvantage is that you need either a sharp knife or the elusive scissors to open them and I, for one, have yet to master the tetrabric-opening art – I inevitably end up with wine or orange juice spurting all over me and the floor!

Wine On Tap

No, not an intravenous drip but a new form of packaging! Bag-in-box wines have taken the wine market by force over the last few years. This ingenious idea came from Down Under, where the Aussies not only perfected the art of bagging their wines but also had the foresight to bag only decent wines. This is where the British wine trade got it wrong. Instead of starting off with decent wine, they bagged anything they could lay their hands on. Because of the expense of the packaging (often more than the base cost of the wine), these low-quality wines were still not cheap and as a result bag-in-box wines received bad press.

Now more people have realised the importance of bagging a quality wine and many companies offer Appellation Contrôlée (an official French quality rating – see Chapter 2, 'Label Fables') French wines in boxes and wines of a similar quality level from other countries. But the Australian bag-in-box still reigns supreme.

If you've never investigated the anatomy of a bag-in-box, it's quite a revelation. Inside the box there is a silver-coloured bag, not dissimilar in looks to a freezer bag. Wine is then dispensed through an ingenious tap which, once mastered, seems to work very well, although a few have a tendency to drip. The marketeers had fully realised the attraction of wine on tap!

While methods of bagging wine are improving all the time, bag-in-boxes have nothing like the shelf life of wine in a bottle, as they are more prone to oxidation. As a result, if you're Winewise, you'll buy your boxes from shops with a high turnover to guarantee their freshness. Until a 'sell by' date is compulsory practice, it is unlikely that any company will take the lead and voluntarily put one on the box.

One of the main advantages of boxes is that they are handy if you just want one or two glasses of wine at a time. Most claim a life of up to three months once opened before the wine starts to deteriorate, but tasting tests have revealed that this does not apply to all bags. Because reds are less prone to oxidation than whites, they tend to keep longer and are the safer bet.

But Winewise buyers should beware. Generally sold in three-litre boxes, wine in a box is unwittingly bought by many people simply because they think it's better value than the equivalent wine in bottle. Because of high bagging costs, this is often not the case, and if you can be bothered to open four bottles rather than having three litres on tap, you'll drink more for less money. Very Winewise! At picnics, barbecues and parties where the corkscrew is bound to disappear anyway, boxes can be good news. They also have the advantage of being much lighter to carry than bottles.

Chapter 2

Label Fables

The King family, according to my mother, had the capacity to understand wine labels well before they could read. That's not to say that we could read them; more that by some child-like intuition, if we were sent to get a bottle from the wine rack, we chanced upon the best bottle almost without exception. Several years later when I started work as a wine writer and tried to understand the intricacies of a German wine label, I realised that my mother must have been right; it can only have been by divine intuition that we chose the right bottles.

And it isn't only children who collect or notice labels. If you keep your eyes open, you too can have some wonderful labels. Look carefully and you'll be amazed what some people choose to call their wines. What exactly has a frost-bitten Blue Nun got to do with wine? Was that what happened to her after she drank it? And fancy having a wine called Cuvée Fanny. Translate the German Krotten-brunnen and discover you're drinking the well of a toad! And Clape just happens to be one of the best Rhône producers. Maybe it's sometimes better not to understand the labels.

But however complicated the label appears, the first most important Winewise thing to look for is the quality level. Wines made in the EEC tend to adhere to the same sorts of classification. Watch out for EEC Tafelwein: it's often disguised in a German-looking bottle but in fact it is a blended wine which can come from any of the EEC countries. It's a way of bottling the wine lake and getting unsuspecting punters to pay for it. It's bland, innocuous and far from exciting.

The most basic quality wines are table wines: Tafelwein

in Germany, Vin de Table in France, Vino da Tavola in Italy. Just above this category are Vin de Pays French wines and the recently introduced German Landwein.

The French have another classification known as Vins Délimités de Qualité Supérieure (VDQS) wines, above Vin de Pays. The next category is what's known as 'quality wines': Appellation Contrôlée (AC) in France, Qualitätswein in Germany, and Denominazione di Origine Controllata (DOC) and also Denominazione di Origine Controllata Garantita (DOCG) in Italy.

Using France as an example, the AC refers to a specific region such as Appellation Bordeaux Contrôlée, a large region which can have several small ACs within it such as AC Pauillac and AC Médoc. As a general rule the smaller the AC, the better the wine.

Always remember that you're paying hard-earned cash when buying a bottle, so it's worth remembering a few of the words that apply to the wines you enjoy – it'll help you make fewer mistakes.

Glossary of Terms

English	French	German	Italian	Spanish	Portuguese
Bottle	Bouteille	Flasche	Bottiglia	Botella	Garrafa
Bottled	Bouteille au château/ domaine	Abfullung	Nel'origine	De origen	Engarrafado na origem
Dry	Sec	Trocken	Secco/Brut	Seco	Seco
Estate	Mis en	Erzeuger-	Imbottigliato	Embotellado	Quinta
Medium dry/ sweet	Demi-sec	Halbtrocken	Abbocato	Semi-seco	Meio seco
Red	Rouge	Rot	Nero Rosso/ nero	Tinto	Tinto
Rosé	Rosé	Rose/ Weissherbst	Rosato	Rosado	Rosado
Sparkling	Mousseux/ méthode champenoise	Sekt	Spumante	Espumoso/ Cava	Espumante
Sweet	Doux/ Moelleux	Suss	Amabile/ Dolce	Dulce	Doce/ Adamado

English	French	German	Italian	Spanish	Portuguese
Table wine	Vin de Table	Tafelwein	Vino da Tavola	Vino de Mesa	Vinho de mesa
Vintage	Millésime	Jahrgang/ Weinlese	Vendemmia	Cosecha	Colheita
White	Blanc	Weiss	Bianco	Blanco	Branco

French Labels

Some other helpful words on French labels include:

Crémant	sparkling but not as frothy as champagne
Cru	from one single vineyard
Cuvée	can be a barrel or vat, and usually indicates a better wine
Demi-sec	medium sweet or medium dry
Doux	sweet
Grand Vin	great wine – often the main wine if a property makes more than one wine
Millésime	vintage
Mis en bouteille au domaine/château	estate bottled
Mis en bouteille dans nos caves	generally bottled by a large company (i.e. not at the estate)
Moelleux	sweet
Mousseux	sparkling or frothy
Négociant	merchant who buys wine, generally bottles it himself before selling it on
Perlé	lightly sparkling
Pétillant	sparkling but less so than champagne
Propriétaire-récoltant	owner/manager
Sur lie	wine left on its lees – natural sediment
Vendange tardive	grapes that are picked late on into the season and result in sweet wine
Vin ordinaire	table wine
Vin tranquille	still wine

German Labels

Despite looking very complicated, German wine labels are probably more logical than most and contain an awful lot of information – too much, in fact! Above Tafelwein are Qualitätswein bestimmter Anbaugebiete (QbA) wines, which will come from a specified region. With German wines the highest possible classification is Qualitätswein mit Prädikat (QmP), after which you'll get the words Kabinett, Spätlese, Auslese, Beerenauslese and Trockenbeerenauslese, all terms which relate to the amount of sugar present in the grape when picked (see Chapter 22, 'Germany').

Abfueller	bottler
Aus eigenen lesegut	producer's estate wine
Eiswein	sweet wine made from frozen concentrated grapes
Erzeugler	producer
Grosslage	large area
Halbtrocken	between dry and medium dry
Perlwein	lightly sparkling
Sekt	sparkling
Trocken	dry
Weinkellerei	winery
Weinzergenossenschaft	growers' cooperative

Italian Labels

Don't automatically write off Vino da Tavola – it can be good, and DOC does not always guarantee a good wine. As ever, the name of the producer is probably the most important word on the label.

DOC	similar to the French Appellation Contrôlée system. There are over 200 DOCs.
DOCG	higher classification and only recently introduced
Abboccato	slightly sweet
Amabile	semi-sweet
Amaro	bitter
Annata	vintage
Asciutto	bone dry
Botte	barrel
Bottiglia	bottle
Cantina	winery
Casa vinicola	wine company
Chiaretto	deep rosé

Frizzante	semi-sparkling
Imbottigliato da	bottled by
Nero	dark red
Reserva	wines with specific ageing
Vendemmia	harvest/vintage

Spanish Labels

Spanish equivalent to the French AC is Denominación de Origen (DO), although again, this is not always a guarantee of quality. But if you're Winewise, you'll check the back labels that state the classification, reserva etc. explained below. Also look carefully for the vintage, which is often in very small type.

Bodega	cellar/where the wine is stored
Clarete	light red
Consejo Regulador	wine governing body
Cosecha	vintage
Crianza	aged
Embotellado por	bottled by
Espumoso	sparkling
Gran Reserva	not sold till five years old with at least two years in barrel
Reserva	wine at least three years old with one year ageing in barrel
Sin Crianza	not aged
Vendimia	vintage/harvest
Viña/viñedo	vineyard

Portuguese Labels

Although Portugal was one of the first countries to classify and demarcate vineyards for port production in the eighteenth century, since then it has lagged behind. Now, slowly more regions are being authorised to put their own names on the labels – but still a lot of the best Portuguese wine is sold as table wine without the name of the region.

Adega	large cellars where wine is bottled
Colheita	vintage
Clarete	light red
Doce	sweet

Demoninação de origem	demarcated region
Engarrafado na origem	estate bottled
Espumante	sparkling
Garrafeira	aged in the bottle
Quinta	farm/estate
Reserva	literally 'reserved' but not always indicative of a better quality

The alcoholic strength of a wine depends on the amount of sugar present when the grapes are picked. The hotter the climate, the higher the potential alcohol. Northern climates such as Germany, which is not blessed with much sunshine, make many light and inoffensive wines, low in alcohol, with around 9 per cent alcohol by volume (you will normally find the percentage on the label).

Most European table wines have around 10–11 per cent alcohol, but some of the top quality French Appellation Contrôlée wines like Burgundy can have up to 13.5 per cent.

Dessert wines such as Sauternes, along with New World wines, can have up to 14.5 per cent.

Most stronger wines have been 'fortified' – i.e. alcohol has been added. These include sherry, port, madeira and Muscat de Beaumes de Venise, with between 15 and 20 per cent alcohol.

Lastly, but not least, if you're Winewise you'll check the bottle size and when comparing price, remember that 75 cl represents 7 per cent more wine than 70 cl.

Hopefully wine labels will become more informative, although if the legislation which some people are pressing for ever gets through, and wine labels have to adhere to the same ingredient listing as food, the Winewise reader is going to need a magnifying glass!

Chapter 3

Vintage Guide
Top of the Year

If you're Winewise you'll remember the vintage – the date on the label which indicates the year the grapes were harvested – of a wine you've enjoyed. And try to remember that a good vintage in one region is not necessarily good in another. The following is a general guide and should be used with care. Because wine is not a constant product there are always exceptions to the rule, so be prepared to experiment – one of the factors that makes it fun becoming Winewise.

In good vintages Bordeaux can produce some of the greatest red wines in the world. They'll often be big, tannic (bitter) wines which need to be kept for a long time until they're softer. Due to modern vinification methods, there has not been a really terrible vintage since 1968, and nowadays even poor vintages tend to produce very drinkable wines.

Excellent: 1986, 1985, 1983, 1982, 1978, 1975, 1970
Good: 1981, 1979, 1976, 1971
Average to Poor: 1984, 1977, 1974, 1973, 1972

Burgundy is far less consistent than Bordeaux because of the large number of producers, the very varied wine-making techniques, and the climate. It is very difficult to generalise and there are exceptions everywhere.

Excellent: 1986, 1985, 1983, 1978, 1971
Good: 1982, 1981, 1980, 1979, 1976, 1972, 1970
Average to Poor: 1984, 1977, 1975, 1974, 1973

The best vintages in Germany are the ones which produce a very high level of natural sugar in the grapes, allowing

the producer to make both great dry wines and sweet wines like Beerenauslese.

Excellent: 1985, 1983, 1976, 1975, 1971
Good: 1986, 1981, 1979
Average: 1984, 1982, 1980, 1978, 1977, 1974, 1973, 1972

Vintage Port is not made every year, and so each year it is 'declared' the quality will be of a relatively high level to start with.

Excellent: 1983, 1982, 1977, 1963, 1955
Good: 1980, 1975, 1970, 1966, 1960, 1958

Vintage Champagne, like Vintage Port, is only declared in good years, and the date of the harvest will be on the label. Non-Vintage Champagne (there won't be a date on the label) is made from a blend from several years. The following vintages have been declared by many Champagne houses in the last ten years: 1982, 1981, 1979, 1978, 1976, 1975.

In countries with hotter climates, the vintage is less important, although it's always an idea to make a note of the vintage of a wine you enjoyed, as there will generally be slight variations.

Chapter 4

A Question of Style

If you've got Winewise style, you'll already know a few tricks of the trade to work out what type of wines you like. Chapter 1 ('Bottle Bulge') has already told you how much (or how little) you can tell about a wine from the shape of the bottle, and this chapter will tell you a bit more about the helpful style codes that most supermarkets use. There's nothing worse than getting home, popping the cork and discovering the wine is too sweet, dry, light or heavy for your taste. Taking note of these codes (where used) can help avoid those embarrassing moments when you offer someone a glass of dry white which turns out to be sweet!

I suppose it's only natural that with white wines outselling red wines in Britain by two to one, coding systems are more commonly used for white wines. But it's also partly because it's easier to differentiate between white wines by assessing their sweetness. Major supermarkets such as Sainsbury's operate a code along the following lines. These helpful 'speaker tickets' (no, they don't actually talk!) and back labels go some way towards describing a style of wine and are generally more helpful than uninterested supermarket shop assistants, the majority of whom are definitely not Winewise. Besides, if used properly, these codes make buying wine more speedy and much more fun.

Dry wines such as Muscadet, Champagne, Chablis and Entre-Deux-Mers are coded number 1 on a 1 to 9 sweetness scale. Liebfraumilch and white Lambrusco are number 5 and very sweet wines such as Sauternes and Muscat de Beaumes de Venise are number 9. This practical coding system makes life less chaotic in the supermarkets and enables you to experiment with more confidence and ease. In addition, supermarket wines often have back labels which describe the style of the wine, tell you where it comes from and suggest suitable foods to accompany it.

Red wines are more complicated to classify because they don't just differ in sweetness levels; it's more a case of light-, medium- or full-bodied. So some shops will use those terms where Beaujolais would be light and fruity, Rioja medium-bodied and Barolo full-bodied and tannic. Along the same lines the Wine Development Board have introduced a similar code from A to E, to be found on the back labels, where As are light and quaffable and Es are bigger and more concentrated with greater depth and fullness.

In independent wine shops you should be able to get advice from the assistant, but it is never a bad idea to know something about styles of wines in case of a non-Winewise assistant.

As a quick reference here's a guide of widely found wine styles.

Whites

Dry, light- to medium-bodied

Alsace
Bordeaux (dry, e.g. Entre-
   Deux-Mers)
Fino Sherry
Frascati
Gros Plant
Luxembourg wines
Mâcon
Ménétou-Salon/Quincy
Muscadet
New Zealand Müller-Thurgau
Pouilly Fumé
Rioja (new style – see chapter
   19)
Sancerre
Sauvignon de Touraine
Sercial Madeira
Soave
Spanish (new style)
Sparkling wines (most Brut
   ones)
Swiss wines
Trocken (Germany)
Vin de Pays

Dry, full-bodied

Chablis
Côte d'Or or white burgundies,
  e.g. Meursault, Chassagne
Graves
Rhône, e.g. Châteauneuf-du-
  Pape

Rioja (old style – see Chapter
  19)
New World Chardonnay/
  Sauvignon Blanc (most)
Vouvray (can be semi-dry)

Medium-sweet, light- to medium-bodied

Amontillado Sherry
Asti
Bual Madeira
German wines up to Kabinett
  quality
Laski Riesling

Liebfraumilch
Monbazillac
Orvieto
Riesling (New World)
Vouvray (demi-sec)

Sweet, full-bodied

Alsace (late-picked)
Cream Sherry
Coteaux du Layon
German wines above Spätlese
  quality
Late-picked wines
Liqueur Muscats (Australian)
Malmsey Madeira

Moscatel de Setúbal
Muscat de Beaumes de Venise
Sauternes/Barsac
Spätlese
Tokay Aszu
Trockenbeerenauslese
Vouvray Moelleux

Reds

Medium-bodied

Bairrada
Bergerac
Beaujolais Crus
Bulgarian Cabernet Sauvignon
Buzet
Chianti
Chilean Cabernet Sauvignon
Clarets (good vintage ones)
Côte d'Or Burgundy
Côtes-de-Francs
Côtes-du-Rhône

Côtes du Ventoux
Dão
Fronsac
Lirac
Navarra
Regaleali
Rioja
St Emilion/Pomerol
Saumur Champigny
Zinfandel (or full-bodied)

Heavy- to full-bodied

Barbaresco
Barolo
Brunello di Montepulciana
Bull's Blood
California Cabernet/Shiraz
Clarets (good vintage ones)
Corbières
Fitou

Madiran
Rhône (better quality ones, e.g.
  Côte Rôtie, Hermitage,
  Châteauneuf-du-Pape,
  Crozes-Hermitage, Cornas,
  St-Joseph)
Rioja

Light-bodied

Alsace
Barbera
Beaujolais (inc Nouveau)
Bourgueil
Chinon
Claret (generic rather than
  specific)

German
Lambrusco
New Zealand
Roussillon
Sancerre
Valpolicella
Vin de Pays

Sweet

Lambrusco (light)
Port (heavy)

Zinfandel (late-picked)

Chapter 5

Converting the Grapes

If you're Winewise you obviously drink wine and enjoy it. And being Winewise doesn't mean you have to know all the intricacies of its making. But if you have a grasp of the basics of wine-making, it can give you sound clues as to why a wine has a particular taste.

Provided the weather is willing, healthy grapes, ripe and without rot, are harvested around September to October in Europe (in the northern hemisphere), and in March in the southern hemisphere. Now, more and more grapes are harvested by huge machines which shake the trunk of the vine, making the ripe grapes fall off. Machines have the advantage that they don't go on strike, don't indulge in the harvesters' well-earned rests and even work all night – particularly important in hotter climates where the grapes oxidise less quickly in the cooler night temperatures. But machines cannot make the selection by hand as trained harvesters do, so it's likely that both methods will continue side by side.

So, once picked, the grapes are taken to the vinification centre, generally close by. They are then crushed and pressed. In white wine-making, the skins are separated from the juice after pressing. To make red wine, the skins are left with the juice for a number of days (depending on the grape and the type of wine required) to give the all-important colour and tannin, a bitter substance also found in tea. It surprises many people to learn that a white wine can be made from red grapes if the juice is taken off the colour-producing skins quickly enough (blanc des noirs champagne is made like this), because the flesh of many red grapes is in fact white. To make rosé, the skins are left in contact with the juice until the required colour is attained.

White wine, once taken off its skins, is generally fermented at controlled temperatures around 15–17°C. By cooling and slowing down the fermentation, the maximum flavour and fresh fruit taste is extracted from the grapes. Traditionally the juice was left to ferment at its own rate, and often the resulting wine tasted hot and boiled, rather like jam.

Red wines are often left with the skins during fermentation and, whilst the temperature is regularly checked so that it doesn't rise too high (above 25°C), reds are not often cooled unless the weather is very hot. Placed either in wooden or, now more commonly, stainless steel vats, red wine fermenting with its skins is a violent process. It's a bit like watching a witch's boiling cauldron. As the wine ferments, the natural sugar in the grape is transformed into alcohol and carbon dioxide.

After fermentation, the winemaker has to decide how to age the wine. Light, clean, fruity whites are often bottled very young, generally about four months after the harvest. Heavy, full-bodied whites (Burgundy, Australian and Californian Chardonnays) and bigger, full-bodied reds (Bordeaux, Italian Barolos and Spanish Rioja) are then left to mature in small, 225-litre oak barrels. These add flavour to the wine. It's more pronounced when the barrels are new, and French and American wood gives the wine very different flavours. New oak often gives off an aroma of vanilla, so if you think you can detect that in a wine, say so – you'll probably be right, and the older the wood, the less pronounced the flavour.

Some of the freshest, fruitiest red wines are made by another method called carbonic maceration. The grapes are left uncrushed in a vat and their pressure and weight inevitably splits the skins of some of them. The juice in the bottom of the vat begins to ferment and the resulting carbon dioxide bubbles between the grapes. With the air excluded, the other grapes begin a sort of 'internal' fermentation (within their skins). This results in lots of black-purple colour being extracted and masses of 'bubblegum'-smelling fruit. But because the skins have not been crushed, little tannin is extracted and the wines made by this method (typified by Beaujolais) are smooth and fruity, suitable for drinking while young.

So if you taste a wine which is bitter and tannic and has a flavour of wood, you'll now be Winewise enough to know the reason why. Generally, heavier, more tannic wines take longer to mature than light, fruity wines, which can be enjoyed the year after harvest. As a wine matures, it slowly loses its hard tannin, which is replaced with much softer-tasting fruit.

But enough of how wine is made. The next chapter is more important – what particular grapes taste like and how to be Winewise enough to tell the difference.

Chapter 6

Grape Expectations
The Fruitful Facts

Now we're getting on to the tasty stuff: what wines actually taste like, and why!

The trendy word in wine talk at the moment is 'varietal', which simply refers to a wine named after a grape variety. It was made fashionable by the Californians, who, once they had jumped onto the wine bandwagon, decided to be as pure as possible.

Single-grape varieties, however, have been in use for some time all over France and Germany. It's simply that few other countries marketed the word. In France the classic Claret area of Bordeaux has always used a blend of grapes, but other regions such as Burgundy traditionally use a single variety for their wines. So neither can be proved to produce the best wines. The most encouraging thing to have resulted from this Californian buzz word is that today more and more producers take the trouble to put the name of the grape on the label. This is all good news for Winewise readers, as you'll be able to follow your grape! But of course, just to make life more difficult, areas such as Burgundy do not name their grapes; they expect everyone to know!

Here, I describe the major single-grape varieties available from several countries and, where they are not mentioned on the label, indicate which wines are made from them. If you like the flavour of a particular grape, for instance Chardonnay, you can look at the table on page 47 to see which wines are made from it. If on the other hand you are bored with the type of wines you are drinking and are looking for a heavier or lighter style, maybe some of the grape variety characteristics described in the next few pages will help you make your choice. (Remember, a wine actually gets its colour from the grape skin, and it is possible to make white wine from red grapes provided the skins are removed from the juice quickly enough.)

The following is by no means a complete list of all the grapes in the world; simply descriptions of those most commonly found on their own.

Whites

Chardonnay This is the sweetheart of the wine world. Everyone tries to grow it. It's understandable, as it does produce some of the most attractive white wines around. It makes rich, dry, whitecurrant-tasting whites, with depth and a buttery, nutty, toasted flavour which is even more marked if the wine has been aged in oak barrels. It has good acidity but does not have the rasping acidity of the Muscadet grape, the Melon de Bourgogne.

Virtually all white Burgundy is made from Chardonnay, although the variety is often not mentioned on the label. There are also several good Bulgarian, Californian, Australian and New Zealand examples which do mention the name on the label. It is now being planted in Italy and in the south of France, where, now that producers have realised its pulling power, they put it prominently on the label. If you buy a Blanc de Blancs Champagne, it means it's made from 100 per cent white grapes, again the Chardonnay.

Sauvignon Blanc This is characterised by its smell of gooseberries and freshly cut grass. Lots of people say it smells like cat's pee, but I haven't got a cat, so I wouldn't know! It makes wines with a flinty, slightly earthy taste, reasonably high in acidity and not as rich or fat as the Chardonnay. In France it is widely grown throughout the central vineyards of the Loire Valley. Just to make things more complicated, the best examples do not state the variety on the label. It's the grape used in Sancerre, Pouilly Fumé, Quincy and Ménétou-Salon from the Loire. It's also used in Bordeaux, sometimes on its own in generic dry whites, blended with another variety, the Ugni Blanc, for Entre-Deux-Mers, and blended with Semillon for white Graves from the Bordeaux region. New Zealand is making excellent Sauvignon Blancs which are good value for money. In California it is often referred to as Fumé Blanc.

Riesling (pronounced Reeceling) People talk about Riesling as smelling oily and petrolly, neither of which, unless you're a car mechanic, sound very attractive. But if you smell a top-quality German Riesling, you'll see what they mean. The smell is rather like oil, but a sweetish, flowery type rather than Duckhams! It's an attractive variety, with medium acidity and good fruit. Wines made from Riesling can be sweet or dry (see Chapter 22), depending on how much natural sugar there was in the grapes. All the best German wines are made from pure Riesling. In Alsace in France they have the right idea. All wines must be labelled with their specific variety. Alsace Riesling is clean, crisp and dry. California uses Riesling (known as Rhine Riesling), to make quite rich, sweeter wines, as does Australia, where it also makes drier versions which are crisp, clean and flowery. One of the commonest forms of Riesling around, though, is Yugoslavian Riesling.

Muscat (definitely not to be confused with Muscadet) This is a very strongly perfumed grape, smelling of sweet peaches. It's used a lot in the Rhône for making a sweet fortified wine, Muscat de Beaumes de Venise. It's also used in south-west France for making large quantities of strongly flavoured wines like Muscat de Rivesaltes. The Muscat grape tends to have a lot of sugar in it, so the resulting wines can be fruity and sweet. But it is also used in Alsace, where it makes a flowery but dry wine.

When used in Australia, the wines tend to be very heavy, thick and sweet (although some producers are making a crisp clean dry variety). The closest comparison is to a Port. If you see the word 'late-picked' on a label, expect an even richer wine. This doesn't mean the grapes were picked in the dead of night, but that they were picked late on into the season when the concentration of sugar was at its highest.

Variations of it are used to make sweet sparkling wines in Italy such as Moscato and Asti Spumante.

Gewürztraminer This is the spiciest white grape variety around. It's used in Alsace and makes a rich, spicy wine. It's also used in Germany, Australia, California and Austria.

Muscadet If you want to impress your non-Winewise friends, you really ought to know that the real name of this grape is the 'Melon de Bourgogne'. Confused? You should be, because Muscadet comes from the Pays Nantais (on the Atlantic French coast) and Burgundy (or Bourgogne) comes from the east (opposite) side of France. There's a story involving shipwrecked sailors from Burgundy bringing vine cuttings to the Pays Nantais which explains this oddity, but whether it's true or not, I don't know. But then again, nor will your friends! It produces dry whites without a distinctive aroma. Muscadets with most character are the 'sur lie' variety, because they derive extra flavour from the lees (natural sediment).

Semillon A white grape capable of producing rich, oily wines which can be dry or sweet with balancing acidity. No, this isn't the description of a garage floor, they can taste delicious! The Semillon is at its best in white Graves, Sauternes (Bordeaux) and Australia. It's often blended with the Sauvignon Blanc and is delicious when fermented and aged in new oak barrels.

Müller-Thurgau Mostly used in high-production German and English wines. A Winewise grape to grow, as it yields big crops and flourishes in cold climates. Not always as Winewise to drink, because it can produce rather bland wines. The best English winemakers have switched to Madeleine-Angevine, Huxelrebe, and more spicy varieties.

Trebbiano This is one of the world's widest-planted grape varieties that disguises itself under a whole host of other names, including Ugni Blanc. It's very prolific, planted extensively all over Italy (used in Frascati), all over the Cognac region, in the Gironde of Bordeaux and in Provence. It's not a particularly interesting grape (the Cognac producers have got the right idea distilling it!) and makes pale, fairly bland wines.

Reds

Gamay This is the 'bubblegum grape', again not generally named on the label. Vast quantities of it are knocked back each year in the form of Beaujolais Nouveau. It's recognisable by its blue-purple colour, smell of bubblegum and fruity taste, the freshness resulting from its high acidity. The natural fruitiness of the grape is enhanced by the way most Beaujolais is made, which does not involve crushing the grapes. Apart from Beaujolais, Gamay is grown in the Loire Valley, and in the south of France in areas like the Ardèche. It's used in many other countries, but mainly for blending. The 'Gamay' used in California is not thought to be true Gamay, but a clone of the Pinot Noir.

Pinot Noir This is the classic red Burgundy grape, again not mentioned on the label. It has a ripe red fruit smell of strawberries and raspberries, with a hint of sweetness even though the wine need not contain any sugar. Sometimes in hot climates or high harvest temperatures it takes on a plummy smell. After ageing in wood, Pinot Noir develops a rich, creamy, strawberry flavour that many people describe as farmyardy, sweet vegetal or gamey. When young, it has good acidity but less tannin and tends to soften out long before block-buster Cabernet Sauvignon-based wines. It's one of the three grapes used in Champagne, and if you see a Champagne labelled 'Blanc des Noirs', it is likely to be made from the Pinot Noir.

Sancerre always used to be a red wine, at least until the region was devastated by Phylloxera, a vine-eating louse, in the late nineteenth century. The red wine was made from Pinot Noir, and there are still some good red Sancerres to be found.

There's also a school of thought that thinks that the Tempranillo grape, used widely to make Rioja, could possibly be a relation of the Pinot Noir. It's not such an outrageous idea, and the really Winewise will compare a bottle of Rioja with a bottle of good Burgundy to find out for themselves.

Cabernet Sauvignon This grape is almost as trendy as Chardonnay. It's the mainstay grape of red Bordeaux but is mixed with other varieties. It smells and tastes of blackcurrants although without sweetness, produces a full-bodied wine with full-flavoured fruit and lots of bitter tannin when young. In Bordeaux it's aged in wooden barrels, which enables some of the best wines to remain drinkable even after a hundred years.

The Californians love it and are making really big, fullblown Cabernet Sauvignon wines. Some innovative producers in Spain such as Torres in Penedès and Raimat in Cataluña are now using Cabernet Sauvignon. But the most popular Cabernet Sauvignon in recent years have been the Bulgarian and Hungarian varieties. For partying and general quaffing this inexpensive tipple is difficult to beat.

Cabernet Franc Used extensively in Bordeaux, this grape could be called the poor relation of Cabernet Sauvignon. It has a much more grassy, stalky smell. If you taste it with your eyes closed, it's not dissimilar to the white Sauvignon Blanc used in Sancerre. It's used on its own in the Loire Valley for wines like Chinon and Bourgeuil and has high acidity with an earthy raspberry flavour.

Merlot Another grape used widely in Bordeaux, especially in St Emilion and Pomerol (see Chapter 17, 'Bordeaux – Without Paying the Dough'). It's also grown successfully in California, where, again, it is mostly blended with Cabernet.

In France, the Merlot makes a soft, fruity wine which sometimes (when vinified badly) produces a vegetal, rotten cabbage-like smell and taste. But at its best it can make wines which are full, fruity and have a flavour of violets (rather like parma violet sweets) ready to drink earlier than those made from Cabernet Sauvignon. It can be a very Winewise grape, provided it's well made.

Syrah (Shiraz) A gutsy grape. In France it makes a full-bodied, fully flavoured wine and is grown mainly in the Rhône valley – look out for Hermitage, Cornas, Côte-Rôtie, St-Joseph and Crozes-Hermitage. It's also grown in Australia. Down under it's called Shiraz and produces strong, spicy, peppery wines. It's often blended with Cabernet Sauvignon to make a more accessible wine.

Grenache Almost exclusively a French grape, this could be called the poor relation of the Syrah. But don't knock it – it makes gutsy wines full of flavour which, even if they are not as refined or complex as those made from the Syrah, can be delicious. What's more, the Winewise will know that they are not expensive. The Grenache features in the wines from the southern Rhône Valley (Côtes-du-Rhône, Côtes du Ventoux, Coteaux du Tricastin) as well as in many wines from the south-west of France. It's also used very successfully in Rioja (Spain), where it's called the Garnacha.

Nebbiolo A big heavy tannic grape used in tarry Italian reds, including Barolo and Barbaresco. Not grown outside Italy.

Zinfandel This is only for the more adventurous Winewise reader. It's a really weird grape grown almost exclusively in California and makes a heavy wine with 'foxy' smells and tastes. If you've got gamey tastes, go for it. But it can also make light fruity Beaujolais-style wines. They've even started making a 'white' Zinfandel. There's just one confusing point here – the wine's pale pink! It's what the Americans call a blush wine.

Grape Types

Grape	Used in following wines
Muscadet	Muscadet (France)
Chardonnay	Burgundy (France), California, Australia, Bulgaria, New Zealand, Chile, Italy
Sauvignon Blanc	Loire (Sancerre, Pouilly-Fumé, Touraine), Bordeaux (Graves, Sauternes), California, Australia, New Zealand
Semillon	Bordeaux (Graves, Sauternes), Australia, New Zealand
Riesling	Germany, Alsace, Australia, California, Yugoslavia, Hungary, England, Chile
Müller-Thurgau	Germany, England, Austria
Trebbiano	Italy, Cognac, Armagnac, Provence
Muscat	Alsace, Rhône, Rivesaltes, Australia, California
Gewürztraminer	Alsace, Germany, Austria, Chile, Australia
Chenin Blanc	Loire (Vouvray), Australia
Gamay	Beaujolais, California
Pinot Noir	Burgundy, California, Australia, Sancerre
Cabernet Sauvignon	Bordeaux, Provence, California, Australia, Bulgaria, Portugal
Cabernet Franc	Bordeaux, Loire (Chinon, Bourgeuil)
Merlot	Bordeaux, California
Syrah (Shiraz)	Rhône, Australia
Grenache	Rhône, south-west France, Rioja
Zinfandel	California

Chapter 7

Tasting
Enough to
Make you Spit!

Wine-tasting must be the only occupation in which it's not thought impolite to spit! While it might appear a rather disgusting, pretentious practice, it does have its uses. Imagine how you'd feel after drinking forty or fifty wines. Legless!

But while the art of tasting seems to have mystique attached to it, there are two simple reasons why it's done: to see if you like the wine, and to ensure it's in good condition. So spitting is essential if you want to taste seriously more than about five wines and compare them, or attempt to be sober enough to remember the taste.

First of all, only fill the glass one-third full. Then take a good look at the colour of the wine by tilting the glass. It's best to do it with good natural light and against a sheet of white paper. By assessing the colour you can tell a great deal about a wine. If it's cloudy, it means the wine is out of condition (or old and hasn't been decanted) and you should return it to the shop or restaurant. Good merchants and supermarkets will have no hesitation in exchanging the bottle, providing you haven't drunk the wine. People who take back empty or almost empty bottles will not receive much sympathy!

Very young red wines are deep purpley-red in colour. As they get older, the colour fades to a tawny browny-red, especially around the rim (the edge of the wine).

White wines become a deeper yellow or even brown with age. Very young whites often have a slightly greenish tinge. Sweet whites tend to be deeper in colour than dry whites.

So, before you've even tasted the wine, if you're Winewise and look at it carefully, you'll already know something about it.

Then take a good sniff. People do this in different ways. Some hold the glass rather precariously to an angle at one side. Others make loud, snorting sniffs! But it doesn't really matter, as long as you can smell something. If the wine has little smell (referred to as 'dumb' or 'closed up'), you can try putting your hand over the top of the glass and shaking it to release some of the aromas. Try not to get wine up your nose – it's easily done!

Often you can tell from the smell alone whether the wine is stable, rather like you can with food if it has gone off. Swirling the wine around the glass helps oxygenate the wine and release the aromas. The aroma or bouquet of the wine can tell you much about its origin even before you've tasted it. From the smell you can often detect the grape varieties used as described in Chapter 6, 'Grape Expectations'.

Then comes the all-important tasting. Take a sip and try to roll it around your tongue so that all the taste buds get a go, as different parts of the tongue can detect different facets of a wine's taste. Again, some people make loud slurping noises rather like a gagging cat! Apart from the flavour, which you should not be shy to describe in whatever words come into your head, things to look for include: acidity level – a sharp prickle on the tongue; the weight of a wine – is it light- or full-bodied? The level of tannin – a bitter substance (also found in tea), and the sweetness or dryness. Often you can detect the way a wine has been aged – a vanilla flavour signifies ageing in oak barrels.

Then try spitting it out. This does take a bit of practice – accurate tasters can spit up to thirty feet. I understand they practise in the bath! Spitting is the only way to remain Winewise if you're tasting lots of wines. One thing to remember: it's not a good idea to spit in a restaurant. Wine waiters get annoyed if their shirts are covered in wine!

I don't know why it is that wine should attract so many pseudo and misunderstood terms. Whether it's because they all originated after drinking a few bottles, or that the terms were thought up by wine snobs who want to perpetuate the mystique I don't know, but there are some real gems! 'Laying down' a wine does not refer to its owner going to sleep, bottle in hand, but rather to laying down the bottle in a cellar and leaving it to mature. When you hear the expression 'travels well', one can well imagine a bottle of wine, either on holiday or cavorting around on a merry-go-round! It means it survived a long trip from where it was made, but today it's hardly relevant because now that transport methods are so reliable, few wines won't travel.

Wines are given all sorts of human attributes, which is not quite as cracked as it may seem, as wine is always a living liquid – continually developing and changing in the bottle. All the human attributes given to a wine are meant to help describe its texture. 'Legs' or 'tears' relate to the alcohol level and the amount of glycerine film evident on the sides of the glass, and 'body' or 'guts' describe how thick or thin the wine is. I haven't heard of a wine with arms, but I'm sure someone will think of it soon! And lots of adjectives are used such as 'unassuming', 'pretentious', 'shy' and 'awkward' which are fine if they mean something to the taster, but don't be fazed by them. If you want to compete, think up some ridiculous-sounding ones of your own!

Letting a wine 'breathe' also sounds ridiculous. Have you ever seen a wine out of breath? But it's the expression used to mean allowing the wine come into contact with oxygen to develop its aroma. Letting the wine 'open up' does not refer

to some magical door-opening bottle but is similar to letting
the wine breathe.

Wines that are described as being 'long' or 'short' can
sound ridiculous but do actually mean something. If you
can still taste a wine long after swallowing it, it's described
as 'long', but if it doesn't have much flavour and leaves no
taste in the mouth, it's 'short'. A wine with 'balance' does
not mean it can walk a tightrope, but that all the elements
of taste are in the right proportions: the fruit, sugar and
acidity. A wine with balance, however, will not necessarily
leave the drinker able to balance if he or she downs one too
many!

And blind tasting has nothing to do with being blind
drunk, but quite the opposite. Blind tasting refers to
tasting a wine and trying to work out what the wine is
and where it comes from. It's quite a fun game, especially
if you taste three wines first, with their labels showing,
then mix up the glasses and see who knows which is
which. Another fun thing to do is to invite guests to try a
red and a white wine either with their eyes shut or while
blindfolded. You'd be surprised how difficult it is, although
most people think they can do it. It certainly beats most
party games I know!

Lots of tactile words are also used for texture, such as
'silky' and 'velvety'. But the majority of wine-tasting terms
relate to the smell and taste of things around us, most
commonly food, especially fruits and spices. And it doesn't
matter how you describe a wine, so long as you can identify
with it. If it smells like a wet dog, say so! Obviously
there'll be others who've never smelt a wet dog or freshly
cut hay and so on, but it's important to use your own
terms.

It's useful to jot down your observations in a book to help
you remember them. But, niceties apart, the main question
about the wine is: do you like it? Taste is very personal and
subjective, and there is no reason at all why one person
should like the same wine as everyone else.

But if this all sounds too pretentious to you, remember
that an awful lot of what is said about wine can be a vin de

load of rubbish and people who go on and on about it are sometimes like a vin de pain in the neck! But the most important Winewise questions to ask are do you like it, and would you buy it? Winewise wise-guys should know!

Chapter 8

What a Corker!

To be really Winewise, you need to be able to drink what's in the bottle! So you don't need to be a mastermind to realise that, as most bottles are sealed with corks, you need a corkscrew. It's only dire emergencies (on trains, or parties when someone's nicked the corkscrew) that call for the age-old trick of pushing the cork into the bottle. This isn't to be recommended, because the laws of hydraulics dictate that a certain amount of the treasured liquid will spurt out all over you, your friends and your furniture. What's more, sometimes the force of pressure is such that the bottle can break. Once, at a party where the corkscrew had disappeared, I tried this method in desperation – the bottom of the bottle cracked, and I was left looking very silly holding an empty bottle by its neck with wine everywhere.

Of course, not all wines have corks – there are screw caps, bags, cans and tetrapacks (which need the ever-elusive scissors and spillage whilst opening is high). But corks are considered preferable for quality wines, even in these high-tech days of plastic wrapping for everything. This is because of the pretentious-sounding expression that wines are living and need to breathe. Imagine a wine gasping for air, suffocating under the screw cap and think how you'd feel – not much of a life! Corks are porous, and have the approval of the Royal Society for Prevention of Cruelty to Wine (patron, Alice King)! But, joking apart, they allow minute quantities of air into the wine which helps its development provided it's not kept for too long. Only some wines are capable of ageing successfully, sometimes longer than humans! But corks can crumble, sometimes with rather expensive results.

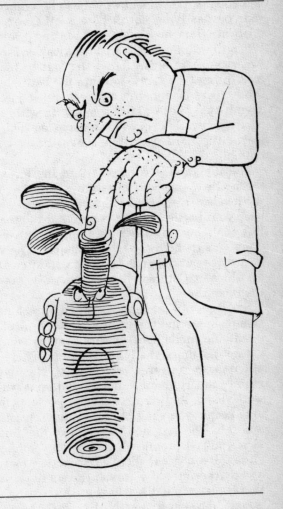

The most dramatic recent event was the sale of a bottle of
1787 Château Lafite-Rothschild which went for the amazing
sum of £105,000 in 1985 at Christie's in London. The
purchaser, a seriously rich American (who owns a magazine
for millionaires), left it standing up in his museum once he

had bought it. Corks have to be kept damp (so always keep your bottles lying down) because they expand when they are wet, thus making a close-fitting seal for the bottle. When they dry out they shrink, with disastrous results. The American gentleman found this out to his cost when the cork in his 1787 Lafite fell into the bottle because, after all those years of hanging on in there, it just could not face drying out. The American ended up with what must have been the world's most expensive bottle of vinegar, and learnt the hard way that that's the way the cookie can crumble!

The ullage of a wine refers to the level of the wine in the bottle. Wine will slowly evaporate over the years, so the levels in very old bottles can be low. It's always best to keep your bottles lying down so that the cork is kept moist. But don't worry, bottles standing up in your kitchen for a week or so will come to little harm. The rate at which a cork dries out depends to some extent on the temperature at which it's stored, but it generally takes years rather than months.

So, to get at that luscious liquid refreshment, you have to rummage around the untidy drawers in the kitchen to find a suitable implement. A corkscrew is what you need, but it's not as simple as it might seem. There are all sorts of different corkscrews, some very effective, some which require superhuman strength, and some which simply don't work. The latter are best used as presents for those unbearable people you can't stand but who insist on sending you presents. The best, and I use one all the time at home, is the 'Screwpull'. I promise I am not on commission from them either. It's a great piece of modern American technology and marketing – if you read the small print on the instruction leaflet you'll discover that the coating used is a type of Teflon developed by NASA for the American space programme.

Its greatest asset is that it is really simple to use, although more difficult to explain. You screw it into the cork and keep on screwing whilst the cork mysteriously rides up the screw and out of the bottle. An American once tried to explain to me the physics of it, but during the explanation I became so interested in the merits of the contents of the rather good bottle he had mistakenly chosen to demonstrate with, that I stopped listening! At the time of writing it is selling for around £9, which might seem like a lot of money, but having used the 'Screwpull' to open as many as seventy different bottles at a time for big wine tastings and survived, I can personally guarantee that this particular corkscrew does not damage your health in any way.

Not everybody agrees with me, though. Some wine waiters think that the 'Screwpull' is only easily usable if the bottle is placed on a table (or a solid surface). In reality this is probably because they enjoy using a Waiter's Friend (one of those metal contraptions with a folding screw and pen-knife), so that they can perform all sorts of contortions whilst struggling to extract the cork. Waiters, well known for their desire to impress (or to intimidate), find the Waiter's Friend a valuable prop in the never-ending quest for one-upmanship. But more of that in Chapter 14, 'Restaurantwise'.

Two other respectable corkscrews are the wooden 'double helix' – it looks rather like a Dalek from Dr Who – and the Italian double-lever, which resembles a space-age version of one of Lowry's stick people.

Butler's Friends are another, rather unconventional, way of opening bottles. If you can get it together (I can't), they are supposed to be excellent. They have two metal prongs which are inserted on either side of the cork. Their nickname is 'wiggle and twist' (no, not a 1960s dance), because of the action needed to withdraw the cork. But the technique is difficult to master, and a fair amount of strength is also needed.

There's one cork extractor that really should be chucked in the wheelie-bin before it puts you in hospital. It works like a bicycle pump – you insert the needle end into the cork and pump away. If you're lucky, the cork glides smoothly out of the bottle because of the air pressure building up inside. But if you're unlucky and the bottle has a flaw, the effect is explosive. You're likely to end up with sharp glass shrapnel in your skin, eyes, or other exposed areas of the anatomy. You won't thank anyone when you are recovering in hospital – it's certainly not an instrument used by Winewise people.

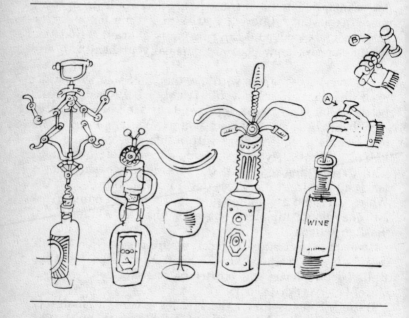

Winewise Yuppies, earning huge sums, will definitely need a pair of champagne pincers to help pop open their bottles of Dom Perignon if one has a reluctant cork. These are like a large pair of nutcrackers used to grip the cork. When opening Champagne (or other fizzy wines), it's always important to remember to turn the bottle around the cork, and not the other way round. This way, the cork is less likely to break.

Exactly how long before drinking a bottle should be opened is often misquoted. While five- to ten-year old Clarets and heavy Italian wines such as Barolo will benefit from being opened and decanted an hour or so before drinking, most wines do not need to be opened until the minute you want to drink them. Little air can get into the neck of the bottle once the cork is taken out, so if you want a wine to benefit from aeration it should be decanted.

Chapter 9

Glass Farce

Drink wine out of exactly what you please, and don't give in to the pompous wine waiters who try to insist on you using a particular glass. People get unduly worried about having the right glass, but again, it's all a bit of a marketing gimmick. Have you ever asked yourself why there are so many different shapes and styles of glasses around? The cynical answer (and one with a certain element of truth) is that the glass manufacturers want to make a living! If they can persuade us all that we must have different wines in different glasses, they are laughing all the way to the bank. So don't be influenced by what they say – make up your own mind and drink out of glasses you like.

Personal preference obviously plays a large part here. I don't go for cut-glass, whether it's the cheap or expensive variety. I like to be able to see what I'm drinking and not have my vision distorted by criss-cross lines. How else can you tell the waiter there is a fly in your wine? If you're assessing the colour of a wine, or trying to see if it is cloudy or full of sediment, a clear plain glass is an asset. Coloured glass is fine if you don't want to see the wine's colour. The basic rule, and one I do agree with, is that wine is best enjoyed out of a material which does not add any flavour. I find that silver goblets, reminiscent of a neo-Gothic horror film, give the wine a nasty metallic taste.

There are certain shaped glasses that I don't find practical. Champagne saucers (rumoured to have been modelled on Marie-Antoinette's breast!) are not good news if you like Champagne. Try walking around with one in your hand, and you'll see what I mean. At least half the contents seem to get spilt unless you have a very steady hand. And if you're drinking Champagne or sparkling wine, it's presumably because you like the bubbles. Saucer-shaped glasses that bring a wide surface of the wine into contact with the

air mean the bubbles disappear much more quickly than they would in a flute-shaped glass. This is my ideal Champagne glass – the bubbles keep on rising for a lot longer than in the saucer-shaped glass. Also, in my view Champagne is a special drink which I enjoy best from an elegant glass.

Glasses with too narrow a neck can be annoying because, if you're trying to smell the wine, very little bouquet can escape, and what's more, those blessed with above average-sized noses could well have a problem! All of which brings us back to the point that you'll enjoy a wine more if you are relaxed with the glass you're using. I don't like drinking out of small glasses; I actually think it makes you drink more. While thimble-sized glasses might be seen to be the right kind of glasses to drink liqueurs from (and they make life easier for restaurants if the glass size corresponds to a measure), I don't much like them. It's more fun to use brandy balloons, even if the standard measure only just covers the bottom.

The weight or thickness of a glass is entirely up to you. I like drinking from fine glass although it tends to get broken much more quickly, especially when washing up. Sturdy glasses are better for rowdy or outside parties. In restaurants they often have different-sized glasses. Although they are as conditioned as we are by the powers of glass manufacturers' advertising, different-sized glasses *do* serve some

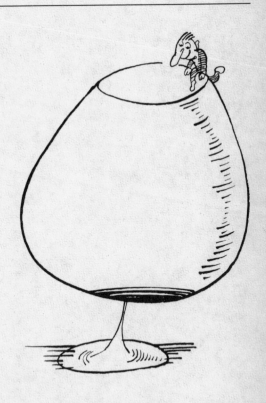

purpose. Two different-sized glasses are an uncomplicated way of distinguishing between two wines. While white wine is often served in the smaller glass, there is no reason why this should be the case. You might wonder why some upmarket restaurants have goldfish-bowl glasses on the table. These are generally used for great red wines, which can benefit from oxidation in the glass. But an ordinary red wine does not always benefit from too much oxidation as it can destroy the fruit, so it's best to keep these for really top wines. Above all, feel Winewise by enjoying drinking out of *your* glasses.

Chapter 10

Decadent Decanters

Wine decanters might conjure up the idea of dusty old bottles, Vintage Port, cellars full of fine wines and pretentious dinner parties. But, believe it or not, they actually have a use for Winewise drinkers. Traditionally decanters were used because, before the days of the cork, most wines were kept in large containers like barrels or even wax-sealed jars. It was unwieldly, as you can imagine, pouring wine out of a barrel. As decanters became more decorative, they acquired a certain snob appeal which soared to ridiculous heights when any wine served had to be in a decanter. The bottle was often never seen on the table.

But times have changed! Most people today are more than delighted to see bottles on the table, and what's more, few people now have a 'Jeeves' on hand to decant their bottles. It's much more likely that today's dinner party wines arrive shaken but not stirred straight from a supermarket trolley. There is little time to open them, let alone search out those decanters you were given for twenty-first birthday or wedding presents. Also, today's drinkers don't tend to have dusty old bottles lying around in their cellars and what's more their friends like to know what they're drinking.

Nevertheless, decanters do have their uses. As with glasses (see Chapter 9, 'Glass Farce'), the style of decanter you like is very much a matter of personal taste. Whereas cut-glass decanters seem to be all the rage for spirits and sherry, I think the best wine decanters are the plainest, although some of the old Georgian ones found in antique shops are very attractive.

In wine-buff circles, to decant or not to decant is almost as hotly debated as nuclear disarmament. In my opinion the main advantage of decanting wine is that, if done carefully, you can enjoy an old bottle of wine without bits of sediment getting stuck in your teeth. Additional pro-decanting arguments are that certain wines, for example young tannic Barolo, generally undrinkable until about ten years old, actually benefit from the oxidation they get when decanted. The air helps to develop the taste and gives the impression of maturing the wine more quickly. So if you have a top quality Bordeaux less than about ten years old, it can often taste better once it has been decanted and left for an hour or two, as the slight oxidation will make the tannin less obvious and the fruit more developed. But the anti-decanting lobby says that, as oxidation is thought to be wine's number-one enemy, decanting is detrimental to a wine's health.

I have witnessed a few decanting tragedies in the past. In many restaurants, wine waiters don't actually know how to decant wine properly, and manage to pour all the very fine bits of sediment into the wine in the decanter, defeating the object of the exercise. Of course if you offer to decant the wine yourself, they generally over-react and look mortally offended.

One time at home a friend very kindly opened one of his good old bottles. With the best of intentions it was decanted half an hour before we were going to eat. But, as with all the best-laid plans, an excess of aperitif Champagne meant the potatoes were forgotten. Once we had remembered them and they were cooked, we sat down with relish to enjoy our generous friend's old bottle. Lunch was by now an hour and a half late and the wine, delicious when first decanted, simply couldn't stand the wait. Too much oxidation had destroyed the taste and the smell of what was a really amazing wine.

So the moral is either make sure lunch is on time, or decant the wine at the very last minute! You can always let it develop in the glass, whereas you can't retrieve a wine whose fruit has evaporated. Remember that it's normally red wines that are decanted, because they benefit from aeration better than whites and they throw a deposit when ten to fifteen years old.

To decant wine properly if it has sediment you have to have a steady hand and a good light. First of all leave the bottle standing up for as much time as you can – at least a few hours. Then, tilting the bottle gently, slowly decant the wine and watch for the sediment which is gradually working its way along the side of the bottle. To do this you can either decant over a candle if you want your kitchen to look like a Hollywood movie set or, more practically, a torch. This enables you to see when the sediment has reached the neck of the bottle. Inevitably you have to leave some wine in the bottle, but I think that's preferable to bits floating around in your glass. If the wine has a lot of sediment and you have to serve it direct from the wine rack, try to keep it horizontal while decanting so that you don't disperse the sediment.

If you want to have fun with your friends, decanters can come in very handy. There is no doubt that people automatically think wine is of a good quality if it is in a decanter. A few years ago I was at a large dinner party where there were two Georgian decanters of red wine on the table and we, the guests, were invited to comment on the wine's origin. Most people decided that it was a fairly good quality claret. Imagine our surprise when the host coolly informed us that the two decanters were actually full of Chilean Cabernet Sauvignon decanted from a bag-in-the-box! So it just shows how misled people can be when seeing a decanter. It's worth trying if you want to catch out any know-it-all friends.

Cool It!

There's nothing worse than drinking luke-warm white or rosé wine; it's far better chilled. Keeping some bottles in the fridge is the obvious answer. But if you're like me and live a totally disorganised life, you never seem to have bottles in the fridge at the right time (although it's true to say that that could be because if they're in the fridge they tend to

get drunk). Anyway know-alls will tell you, quite rightly, that if wine is too cold it masks the aroma and flavour. So, when you take a bottle of white out of the sticky car, what do you do with it in the half an hour you have before your guests arrive? One of the easiest solutions (unfortunately) requires having been organised enough to refill your ice tray. Then you can prise the ice cubes out of their tray and put them in an ice bucket if you've got one (but a plastic bucket or washing up bowl will do even if it's less elegant). The trick is to fill the bucket with cold water as well as ice cubes, as this cools the wine much faster than ice cubes alone.

For non-fillers of ice trays, there are a few ingenious wine cooler inventions on the market. The best actually chills the wine rather than keeping it chilled. It's a Swiss brainwave, and involves four slim plastic freezer-packs (not dissimilar to those used in picnic boxes) that are inserted between the bottle and the wine cooler. As long as you remember to put these in the freezer in between use, they will chill a bottle of wine in about half an hour. In addition they are more elegant and less messy than chilling wine in ice and water.

If you're highly organised and you already have the wine nicely chilled in the fridge but want to ensure it doesn't get warm whilst serving, try using a perspex 'Vinicool' which will keep the wine cool rather than actually cooling it. It works on the same principle as double-glazing!

Getting the Temperature Right

So far, only white wines have been discussed. But there is no reason why you shouldn't drink red wines chilled if you want – indeed, lighter wines such as Beaujolais and Loire reds are often very pleasant served chilled as the producers drink them. In fact the whole concept of serving red wines at room temperature is somewhat invalid, because when the idea was first thought of, it was long before the advent of twentieth-century central heating. So room temperature used to mean almost chilled. Drinking warm red wine in hot smoky wine bars is pretty unpleasant. In fact, if a wine is too warm it destroys its aroma and taste. So if you're in a restaurant and the red wine is almost burning your tongue, ask for an ice bucket, ignoring the sneering wine waiter who is obviously not as Winewise as you are.

This happened to me in a trendy London restaurant while I was with the editor of one of the major glossies. Having ordered the wine, I was a little concerned by its taste. Much to the disgust of the wine waiter, I asked for an ice bucket. Once cooled down, the wine was much improved and the editor somewhat amused. Remember, if you're paying the bill (actually in that case I wasn't!) you ought to be able to drink your wine at whatever temperature you like. I for one would always prefer a wine to be too cold rather than too hot.

Sometimes red wines can be much colder than you'd like. The best remedy for this is to put them in a bucket of hot water. Some people take twentieth-century technology too far by putting the magical microwave to the test. While a few experiments have not proved that this destroys the wine, I wouldn't recommend it. A much less hazardous method is to pour the wine and simply hold the bowl of the glass in the palm of your hand. Hot-blooded Winewise readers will easily warm up their wine.

Chapter 11

Cupboard Love

So you've bought a few bottles (well, more than you need for this evening, anyway) and you've discovered the problem of having nowhere to put them. Today few houses have underground cellars and the very mention of a cellar conjures up ideas of huge vaulted underground rooms with thousands of dusty bottles. Most of that (including the spray-on cellar dust sold in America) really isn't necessary, except for keeping fine wines for a long time.

In fact a cellar can be anything you want it to be, from the cupboard under the stairs, a wine rack, the garden shed, the wardrobe, or even under the bed! On a much shorter term a 'cellar' is really wherever you choose to put the bottles until they're drunk. You don't need anything grand. Many supposedly 'grand' cellars have their problems too – lots are damp, and some are even prone to flooding. In my father's cellar, snails took a fancy to the glue on the labels and simply had a feast!

There are lots of good wine racks around, both small and large, which will fit in anywhere you'd like them. Many can be made to fit whatever space you have, or handy people (myself not included!) often make their own. For wines you're not going to keep for a long time, the exact temperature of where you keep them is not really too important, although it's Winewise to avoid wide extremes of temperature.

In our house we have a separate drinks fridge (my mother's old one) which is generally much fuller than our food fridge! A fridge is not a bad place for whites and rosés, although try to ensure you don't chill the flavour out of them. You can also buy special wine fridges which are supposed to keep the various wines at exactly the right

temperature. But they are expensive and best left for
wealthy restaurateurs.

Larders, pantries or cupboards-under-the-stairs are all
fine for mini wine cellars, again, particularly ones where
the temperature doesn't vary much – airing cupboards are
a bit too warm!

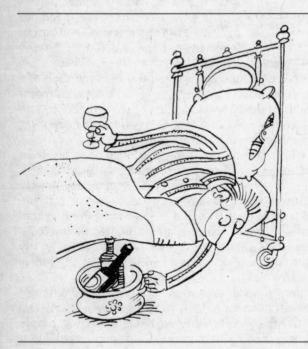

Those who have lots of bottles and are determined to have
an underground cellar can build their own. There's an
excellent one on the market at the moment known as 'the
spiral cellar'. It can be built anywhere where the water
table is not too high. Basically it works by digging a hole at
least six feet deep, inserting a strong plastic liner and then
building a spiral staircase which has holes for bottles
underneath the steps. It's quite effective, but costs a few
thousand pounds.

When people think of creating a cellar, they tend to imagine they've got to buy only fine wines which need laying down for years until they're ready for drinking. But a good cellar will have a balanced choice for current drinking and, if well selected, means you don't have to dash out to your nearest shop every time you have an unexpected guest. It's often a good idea to buy a few bottles or a case of any wines you particularly like, as shops change suppliers regularly and vintages also continually change. If you're Winewise, you'll always have a few bottles up your sleeve (or even in the broom cupboard) for impromptu occasions – generally the most enjoyable.

Chapter 12

Bottle Stop

It's no good knowing what to buy if you don't know where to find it. So Bottle Stop is the Winewise whistle-stop tour which puts on the map the best places to shop.

Wine snobs might sneer at supermarkets, but they're simply not Winewise enough to know what they're missing. Buying wine from supermarkets has never been so good, and because of such successful sales leading to huge buying power, they are able to offer competitive prices on many wines. But in the wine writers' scramble to write about wines available nationally, many of the hard-working independent wine merchants sometimes get forgotten. If you're Winewise, you'll buy from both, for they each play an important role. While supermarkets can be the most competitive, they often require too high a quantity to list the more individual wines made in small amounts.

Super Supermarkets

Sainsbury's Sainsbury's are deservedly top of the list and account for higher sales than all the other supermarkets (they have around 270 stores). All Savacentres, a joint venture between Sainsbury's and British Home Stores, stock Sainsbury's wines. Their range is impressive, both in the quality and quantity of wines on offer.

Right across the board their range of over 200 wines offers sound commercial value for money from their cheapest Vin de Table wines to the finer wines in their vintage selection. Sainsbury's own-label wines, particularly the cheaper ones, rarely disappoint, as they seem to be just a touch sweeter than other generic examples. France, Germany and Spain are well covered and Sainsbury's Portuguese red wines are well worth searching out. They were to some extent the instigators of the current influx of Portuguese reds into this country.

Their own-label Champagnes, non-vintage, vintage and rosé, continually come out well in blind tastings. In addition, the rest of the Champagnes on offer are always competitively priced.

And their selection of French country wines such as Bergerac, Buzet and Fitou is particularly good value. Watch the vintage selection, as it is constantly changing and they sometimes buy smaller parcels of wine for this section. But don't automatically assume that the best wines will always be those with the vintage selection seal on the label.

Take notice of the 1–9 sweetness scale used for the white wines and take the trouble to read the helpful back labels. You'd be amazed how easy it is to become more Winewise with a little bit of extra information.

Waitrose Waitrose probably offer the most unusual wines, and often go for distinctive flavours rather than a universally pleasing generic taste. Waitrose have an advantage in that they have far fewer stores (around eighty) than Sainsbury's, and therefore buy smaller and sometimes more interesting parcels of wine. But they do offer as many as 250 different wines.

Price for price, they are generally very similar to Sainsbury's, but because their wines are selected for their distinctive character, you might find some that aren't to your taste. But for every one you don't like, there'll be more than one which you'll love.

Waitrose are particularly good on French country wines, Australian wines, Spanish and Italian (they even have a good Sicilian wine, Regaleali). Very sound wine-buying goes on here, complementing the quality food. If you do notice that a wine is slightly more expensive than its supermarket competitors, it's generally worth it.

Try their own-label Champagne and experiment with the

impressive range of some of the more unusual sparkling wines.

Tesco Tesco have over 330 shops, and are thought to be fast on the heels of Sainsbury's, the market leaders. Again, they offer a very wide range, often with some of the most competitively priced generic wines around. They seem particularly good at bagging and tetrapacking (similar to orange juice cartons) decent wines – so many others put really duff wine in to start with and then wonder why the wines get so slated by the press. They are generally up there with, if not before, competitors Sainsbury's in introducing new lines. Spanish and Portuguese wines seem to be good value on their list at the moment. Sometimes the quality of their more expensive Fine Wines is less impressive.

Marks and Spencer's Their wines are generally marginally more expensive than the last two stores and the range is much smaller. All products in Marks compete for shelf space depending on how much they sell, so the area given over to wine is not always very large. They sell lots more underwear! But quality control is high, and wines rarely disappoint. They've recently launched several new own-label wines, particularly from Italy.

Their own-label Champagne has always been good. Generally it's of a richer style than other own-label examples. Buying wine from Marks is a good idea for first-time buyers who might not want to be confronted with a huge range.

Asda Nowadays you can buy almost anything at an Asda superstore (even a Mazda at Asda), and more recently a really impressive range of wines. The dynamic wine buyer has totally revamped the range and slapped on designer labels. If your Winewise friends don't like seeing a supermarket name on a label, Asda have kept theirs in small print. They often manage to have some of the cheapest wines around, although it pays to check the bottle size; remember that a 75 cl bottle contains 7 per cent more wine than a 70 cl bottle.

Their Champagne is always worth a go as is their good value, albeit limited, range of New World wines. Spanish wines and French Vin de Pays wines are exceptionally good value.

Hilliards A northern chain of supermarkets which until very recently offered a distinctly non-Winewise selection. Now this one hundred-year-old family company has been given a new lease of life by a new wine buyer. Wines are characterised by their upfront fruit and are always well made examples. The range is expanding all the time and prices are keen to match the local competition.

Morrisons Another northern chain with a good selection across the board. Lots of interesting French regional wines as well as an increasing range of Spanish and Italian wines. Good clarets, although less good on the Burgundy front.

High Street Chains

Oddbins Despite the recent takeover by the biggest liquor company in the world, Seagrams, Oddbins have managed to retain their varied and interesting list. There are currently about 100 Oddbins stores, and it's the derivation of their name and the whole philosophy behind their conception which makes them a Winewise shop. They often buy up odd parcels (or bins) of various wines which makes shopping there more interesting. But it can be frustrating if a wine you like appears and disappears before you've had time to buy in enough stock.

They tend to be ahead of the game in several new wine-producing areas, and don't just select a few token wines. For example, they've currently got over thirty Australian wines, and a really good Portuguese and Spanish selection. They're good on malt whiskies and Armagnac and offer a reasonable selection of clarets. Prices are often discounted and sometimes they offer seven bottles for the price of six. If all High Street specialist wine shops had such a good choice, life would be a lot easier for the non-Winewise drinker. And what's more, you're likely to encounter helpful and friendly service at Oddbins, not a common occurrence at many supermarkets and wine shops.

Peter Dominic Sound wines here, but the selection varies greatly in different branches. Rarely the cheapest, they do offer some good value wines which one would expect, given the size of the chain (480 shops). Since taking over Bottoms Up stores, the Spanish and Portuguese sections are greatly improved and French regional wines offer a good selection. And they've made something of a speciality of malt whiskies.

As with other large off-licence chains, it's not only the selection that varies from shop to shop – so do the staff. While you'll find some friendly and helpful, others are definitely not Winewise at all. In fact, I doubt they know what it means!

Victoria Wine The biggest of the off-licence chains with over 850 shops. Some of the wines are very cheap, but not always of the best quality. Size of shop and selection is often a problem, as smaller shops stock few wines and lots of beers and spirits. However, they have got some good French Vin de Pays wines, and in their largest stores stock a reasonable selection of wines from around the world.

Peatling and Cawdron A chain of shops in East Anglia with one of the best selections of middle-priced good quality wines. Peatlings still bottle some of their own-label wines in England, and although this has become very unfashionable, they keep a beady eye on the quality. As a result, some of their petit château clarets are particularly good value. Because they buy and store the wine themselves until it is ready for drinking, they're one of the few chains with mature wines on the list. Owned by brewers Greene King, they have invested money in wine stocks in the past and Winewise drinkers in East Anglia (they're hoping to open in London soon) ought to get to know their shops.

The Market Situated in London, these seven shops are run by Britain's Italian wine messiah Nick Belfrage. So as well as offering probably the most comprehensive (and best quality) Italian wines around, they also have good value wines from the rest of the world.

Davisons One of the best chains of wine shops in London and the south, Davisons are still a family-run business who know how to buy wine. For years they have bought clarets and Burgundies *en primeur* (see Chapter 17, 'France', p.124), and as a result can offer relatively mature vintages. They've got a good range of wines from all around the world and you're lucky if you've got a Davisons nearby.

Fullers A chain of over fifty shops in London and the home counties. Owned by the brewery Fuller, Smith and Turner, they have recently turned their attention to wine and now have a wide range of well-chosen wines in addition to their own well-respected beers and spirits. And while they are not as well known as other larger brewery-owned chains, the wines are more Winewise. But shops vary in size and you may be unlucky and find uninterested staff running them, some of whom are definitely not Winewise. The bigger shops stock over 350 wines and good value can be found among the regional French wines.

Interesting Independents

Adnams, The Crown, Southwold, Suffolk
(tel: 0502-724222).
Adnams produce what is rated to be one of the most impressive coffee-table wine lists, and the wines aren't bad either! Run by Simon Loftus, who has very definite ideas about wine, there's a good range of wines from all the best areas, including both traditional and New World alike. If you want to try any of their wines, make a special effort to visit The Crown at Southwold, where you can buy several by the glass from a Cruover machine (which keeps the wines fresh under inert gas) at the bar. Or you can choose

from the very impressive wine list in the restaurant, where the standard mark-up of a few pounds per bottle makes choosing mind-boggling for the Winewise reader. Apart from their shop in Southwold, Adnams operate a mail-order service all over the UK.

Domaine Direct, 29 Wilmington Square, London WC1
(tel: 01-837 3521/1142).
Quite simply the best Burgundy suppliers around, and not to be confused with companies of similar names. They know all their wines and growers inside out, and if you can keep up with the speed at which Simon Taylor-Gill speaks, you'll very soon be Winewise about Burgundy or at least certainly well on the way.

Hilary Gibbs, the mastermind behind the company, is as helpful but doesn't speak quite so fast! They hold regular tastings for their customers, and although they supply many hotels and restaurants, they sell to the public as well by the case, which can be mixed.

Farr Vintners, 154 Tachbrook Street, London SW1
(tel: 01-630 5348).
Fine wine dealers who sell unsplit cases only. A selection of top Burgundies at very competitive prices and lots of old and rare Bordeaux. If they haven't got a fine wine you want, they'll generally know where to find it at a reasonable price.

Hungerford Wine Company, 128 High Street, Hungerford, Berkshire
(tel: 0488-83238).
This company is 'amazing', or so I'm told by the eccentric owner known throughout the trade as 'Billy Whizz'. This isn't just because he's a paid-up subscriber to the Beano, but because of the speed with which he dashes around the love of his life, Bordeaux. And I should know, because I'm married to him!

I'm told by other wine hacks and hackettes that he's got a good range of young clarets and not a bad selection of wines from the rest of the world. One of his specialities is *en primeur* Bordeaux offers, which have a very wide following. But I'll leave the Winewise reader to investigate this further, for I wouldn't like to seem biased in any way.

Sales are by the bottle from the shop in Hungerford or mail-order throughout the UK.

Lay and Wheeler, 6 Culver Street West, Colchester, Essex (tel: 0206-67261).
Lay and Wheeler, along with Adnams, produce one of the finest lists in Britain, and offer a particularly good selection

of Bordeaux and Burgundy. They buy well across the range
and offer exciting wines at reasonable prices. You can either
visit one of their shops in Colchester, or buy mail-order
through their list.

Each year they hold a series of wine workshops, tutored
tastings and dinners, often where the proprietors are present. They're informative and thoroughly enjoyable, great
news for Winewise readers.

Ostlers, 63a Clerkenwell Road, London EC1
(tel: 01-250 1522).
Run by an Australian winemaker, Ross Sheppard, this shop
possibly offers the best selection around of Australian
wines. They have just about every grape variety you can
imagine. And now they've added over sixty wines from the
USA – California, Oregon and New York State. They've got
decent French wine, too.

In addition, they run a very Winewise wine appreciation
course with tastings throughout the year. These are
designed to be fun as well as informative, and with Ross
Sheppard at the helm, are bound to be.

Reid Wines, The Old Mill, Marsh Lane, Hallatrow, Bristol,
    Avon
(tel: 0761-52645).
Run by Bill Baker and Charles Reid, a couple I once
accurately described as the Tweedle Dum and Tweedle Dee
of the wine trade, this company probably offers the most
comprehensive selection of fine and rare wines in Britain.
So if you want to buy a special bottle from somebody's birth
year, whatever their age Reid's can usually find you something. And what's more, they've generally tasted them all
personally and are refreshingly honest about the wine's
condition.

It's one of the most enjoyable wine lists to read because of
a series of funny wine quotations and Bill Baker's informed
and fairly candid opinions.

Howard Ripley Wines, 35 Eversley Crescent, London N21
(tel: 01-360 8904).

Howard Ripley is a one-off. He is a dentist and wine enthusiast *extraordinaire*. He has been extremely Winewise for years (though he's still young – in his forties) and his cellar is the envy of many wine lovers. Now, fortunately for the Winewise reader, he's started a wine business which he runs from home. This includes a fine range of Burgundies, many from small growers, that others in the wine trade can't get hold of. And it's not just the well-known names. Knowing the Burgundy region as he does, Howard manages to secure parcels of growers' basic wines which taste as if they cost twice the price.

His typewritten list also includes classics from his own cellar with lots of mouth-watering clarets. Like the best fanatics, Howard Ripley has always been more than generous in sharing his best bottles with Winewise friends. And he is more than adequately qualified to give extremely Winewise advice to customers. As he is looking into mouths all day long in his surgery, it's best to telephone him in the evening or at the weekend if you want advice.

Sales are by the case only, mail order throughout Great Britain.

La Vigneronne, 105 Old Brompton Road, London SW7
(tel: 01-589 6113).
Situated in London's Old Brompton Road, this is the only wine shop I know of where a parrot contributes to the definitely Winewise conversation! It's one of the most interesting wine shops in London, offering good value across the board, particularly in the middle-price range, and you can buy single bottles. It makes a speciality of old and rare bottles but there's masses of choice of reasonably priced wines for everyday drinking.

Run by Liz and Mike Berry, one of the most Winewise events that La Vigneronne organise is their twice-weekly tastings for less than the price of a good bottle. This is the kind of Aladdin's cave where you can seek down-to-earth advice and where the choice appears never-ending.

This entrepreneurial couple have now started up a separate company (L'Alsacien) specialising in the top wines of

Alsace. To keep prices competitive, sales of the Alsace wines
are by the case only, although this can be mixed.

Yapp Brothers, The Old Brewery, Mere, Wiltshire
(tel: 0747-860423).
Former dentist and doctor respectively, this husband and
wife team quite simply have the best Rhône and Loire wines
around. Yapp's wines have never been cheap, but the
quality speaks for itself (although Robin loves talking!) and
the list does a lot more than that. One of Robin Yapp's great
skills is his ability to describe in graphic, poetic detail the
characteristics of his rustic producers. In addition, he's got
some of the best Provençal wines around, and his Champagne Jacquesson is one of the finest.

Wine Warehouses

Majestic Wine Warehouses An appropriate name for the
company who have put wine warehouses on the map. They
are a young zippy company, who have dispelled many of the
cobwebs the traditional wine trade has taken years spinning
about wine. They pile wine high in bare boarded warehouses, give customers the chance to taste before they buy,
provide car parks and have young knowledgeable staff. All
of which is extremely good news for the Winewise reader.
They've recently done a David and Goliath take-over of a
huge chain of stores in the United States which makes them
the biggest independent drinks retailers in the world, so
they can now buy even more competitively and have a
fabulous range of Californian wines.

Winewise buys go right across the board, from their
exceptionally cheap, sound table wines to top-class clarets.
And in between there are 1000 other wines which come
from all the Winewise region. Sound, Winewise buying goes
on here and the quality is good. Sales are by the case only
(which can be mixed). Get a copy of their chatty informal
list and study it before you buy or drop into one of the
twenty branches around the country and see what they have
on offer for tasting.

Chapter 13

Auctions
Sometimes a
Winewise Bid

Buying wine at auction can be a good bet, but a certain amount of skill is involved too. Generally at the big auctions you're bidding against the wine trade and dealers from around the world. But that isn't necessarily bad, because one could argue that if they're prepared to pay the price for something it can't be such a bad buy, as they are obviously going to sell it on. However, they often have customers who require a certain wine, whatever the price.

Christie's and Sotheby's are the two main auction houses, which not only hold auctions in London but also occasionally around the country. Make sure you get hold of a catalogue first so that you can do your homework and don't end up paying over the odds for a wine that you could have bought more cheaply elsewhere. At the biggest sales there are often pre-sale tastings, so you can actually get to taste the wine you might be bidding for. If you're unable to get to the auction yourself, you can leave a commission bid with the auctioneer specifying the maximum you're prepared to pay.

Be careful to take note of the exact quantities you're bidding for. Often eleven-bottle cases come up at auction when the original owner has opened the case, tried the first bottle and not liked it. But that's not to say that it's not a good wine. Unfortunately there's no hard-and-fast rule.

It's essential that before the auction starts you've already determined the maximum price you're prepared to pay for any wine. It's all too easy to get caught up in the auction fever and imagine that just one more bid will secure you the wine. Be fairly wary about the 'reserve' prices given in the catalogue. These are generally the lowest price at which the vendor is prepared to sell, so often the actual selling price is substantially more. Many a punter has come a cropper or at least gone home disappointed because the wines he planned to buy at bargain prices were sold for far above their reserves.

Christie's, in South Kensington, London SW7, hold some interesting 'inexpensive and everyday drinking wines' sales which cover all sorts of wines, including bankrupt stock. At these auctions you can often find Winewise bargains and can generally taste the wine before the sale.

Don't be frightened of bidding; it's really quite fun. As a child I often used to go with my mother to country house sales. On one occasion the marquee was so packed that the only place I could find to put my four-year-old body was underneath the auctioneer's table. He couldn't quite under stand why the whole of the room were grinning like Cheshire cats until his assistant explained to him that I had been bidding (out of his view but in full view of the room) thousands of pounds for a fairly substantial parcel of port. In future my mother always found me a chair. I can remember being too nervous to scratch my nose or wink an eye for fear of the wooden hammer descending, but in reality it's nothing like as panicky, and if an auctioneer isn't sure whether or not someone is bidding, he generally asks them.

Beware of 'buyers premium', which can be as much as 10 per cent plus VAT on top of the hammer price. The seller or vendor also has to pay the standard auction house commission.

Make sure you check whether or not the wine is 'duty paid' or 'in bond', as if it's the latter you'll have to pay the duty, currently £8.82 a case. If it's fine wine you're buying, try and find out where and for how long it has been stored. If it's been standing upright in a shop window for twenty-odd years or languishing in the greenhouse, it's unlikely to be in very good condition. And if you're buying very old wines, check out the ullage (the level of the wine in the bottle). If it is described as being 'mid-shoulder', it's possible the wine will not be in very good condition.

If when you get the wine home and taste it you find that it's faulty, call the auction house immediately. Their reaction depends to some extent upon exactly what was specified in the catalogue, but often they will undertake to make enquiries with the vendor. But you will have to take a chance if you are buying it to lay down, so get as much advice as you can before you bid.

At the end of the day, buying wine at auction is a gamble, but one which can pay off. But you can never be 100 per cent sure, and if the price is not that competitive, you're better off buying from a reputable wine merchant.

Auction Houses

Christie's, 8 King Street, London SW1Y 6QT
(tel: 01-839 9060).

Christie's, 63 Old Brompton Road, London, SW7
(tel: 01-581 2231).

Sotheby's, 34–5 New Bond Street, London, W1
(tel: 01-493 8080).

International Wine Auctions, PO Box 760, London
   SE1 9DB
(tel:01-403 1140).

Philips, Son and Neil, 39 Park End Street, Oxford,
   OX1 1JD
(tel: 0865-723524).

Colliers, Bigwood and Bewlay, The Old School, Tiddington,
   Stratford-upon-Avon, Warwickshire, CV37 7AW
(tel: 0789-69415).

Lacy Scott, 1 Cornhill, Bury St Edmunds, Suffolk,
   IP33 1BA
(tel: 0284-67121).

Chapter 14

Restaurantwise

Have you ever tried ordering wine in a restaurant and wished you were more Winewise? In this chapter I'll tell you how.

In general wine waiters are a pompous bunch, and if you don't want them to spoil your meal, you need to be able to handle them. Relax, don't panic and remember they're there to add to your enjoyment, not wreck your meal.

You need to be able to find your way around the wine list. The reds and whites are normally on separate pages, and are generally listed under the headings of country and region. Some restaurants even list the wines under style, making it easier to choose the right wine.

But how do you judge a good wine list? First of all, a long wine list does not necessarily mean it's going to be good. Anyone can buy fifty or one hundred wines just to make it look impressive. It's the information that you want that will help you find the right bottle. The more information the better – '1985 Côtes-du-Rhône Villages, Paul Jaboulet Aîné' is much better than just 'Côtes-du-Rhône', because it tells you the vintage and the producer's name. In the Côtes-du-Rhône area alone there are several hundred winemakers, all making unique wines of different qualities, all sold under the generic name 'Côtes-du-Rhône'. Some good wine lists will also have helpful descriptions of the wine's taste.

The well-known brands rarely represent good value (you're paying for their massive advertising budgets), and the Winewise reader will often choose a house wine instead, which can offer better value. Also remember that a good house wine will indicate a wine list chosen with quality as an important factor. Never be ashamed of ordering the house wine, even if the wine waiter implies that you are making a downmarket choice – he's just trying to sell you a more expensive wine to increase profits.

There are too many wine lists which only feature well-known names like Sancerre, Chablis, Meursault or Chianti. An adventurous restaurateur will always try to provide a lesser-known and better-value alternative. For instance, instead of Sancerre try Quincy, Ménétou-Salon or Reuilly, which provide equally good-quality and similar-style wine at far less money; for Meursault a good Auxey-Duresses can be comparable; and instead of Chianti, Tignanello is often far better quality.

If the wine waiter does not show you the bottle before it is opened, you are entitled to throw a tantrum. For a start, the restaurant could have re-bought the wine with a new vintage (not the one shown on the list) which might not be as good as the wine you ordered. Or he could have misheard you and selected the wrong wine – and then tried to blame you for the mistake. Or, worse still, an inferior wine could be decanted into an empty bottle (of the wine you chose) and passed off as being the same.

Some waiters try to plug their nostrils with the cork – or so it seems when they smell it. This is a totally unnecessary ritual, and I can't think why they still do it!

Then, when you're asked to taste the wine, accept the challenge. Look at the colour – if it's cloudy, there's likely to be something wrong with it and you are probably entitled to ask for a fresh bottle. But if there are bits or crystals in it, this probably means that the wine has not been properly decanted and you can console yourself with remembering that the bits will probably not harm you. Crystals are virtually never harmful – they just get stuck between your teeth and add nuisance value! Then smell the wine (swirling it in the glass will release some of the aromas and make it easier to smell), remembering that, as with food, if you smell something really unpleasant, like a corky smell in the case of wine, there is likely to be something wrong with it. But don't get this confused with the individual character of the wine itself.

Now take a mouthful of the wine (but don't spit it out – it's unlikely to make you popular) and roll the wine about in your mouth. Again, assess the wine and see if you think it is acceptable. The main fault in any wine that you are likely to taste in a restaurant is that it might be corked. This doesn't mean that there are bits of cork floating in the glass, but it does mean that there is a distinct smell and taste of mouldy cork in the wine. If you are certain that this is the case, you are justified in sending the bottle back and asking for a new one. But even the very Winewise person can encounter difficulties in this apparently simple operation. There are too many wine waiters who don't even know what a corked wine is if they are shown one, and who can become quite aggressive if they think that you are wrong.

There is a lot of nonsense talked about the temperature at which a wine should be served, but there is a certain amount of truth in some of what's said. Too cold (whether it's red or white) and you won't be able to detect any of the subtle nuances of smell and taste of the wine. Too warm, and the wine can taste as if it has been boiled and stewed. Serving at room temperature is one of the greatest fallacies in winespeak. The phrase was invented before central heating was, and room temperature in those days was certainly not that warm. Anybody who overheats a wine is likely to ruin it irretrievably.

However, if a white wine is served too cold, it can be warmed by cupping the glass in your hand and swirling it around gently. And a good way to correct the temperature of a red wine served too cold is to ask for an ice bucket full of warm water and to put the bottle in it for a few minutes. You might get some raised eyebrows from stuffy wine waiters, but you're paying for the bottle, and why shouldn't you drink it at the temperature you enjoy?

There's a moral to this story: beware of pompous wine waiters and don't be taken in by them. Often they know less about wine than you do. In a trendy restaurant in London's Covent Garden a French wine waiter informed me 'zat Bordeaux and Burgundy are ze same wine from ze same region. I should know,' he said, 'because I am French.' When I last looked at a map they were 300 miles apart, but what do I know, I'm not French!

Chapter 15

Food and Winewise

There are lots of rules telling you which wines to drink with which foods, and the best policy is to ignore them. If you enjoy drinking a white wine with your beef, a red wine with your pudding, or a sweet wine with your starter, go ahead and do that. Ignore any disapproving comments – 'Is Sir/Madam really sure that that's the right choice?' – and insist on *your* choice. After all, in Sauternes itself it is very common to drink Sauternes throughout the entire meal with every course. If the people who make the wine can do that, why can't you?

But having said that the rules are there to be broken, it is helpful to have a general idea of what wine goes best with which food. So here's a table to help you, but remember that the final choice is yours – bend the rules as much as you like!

Food	Wine
Plainly cooked fish or white meat	Mostly dry whites – Loire, Burgundy, Friuli, Graves, Alsace, German Trocken, new-style white Rioja, Muscadet, Champagne, Cava.
Spicy seafood and white meats	Spicy Alsace (like Gewürztraminer), Sauternes, sweet Vouvray, old-style white Rioja, Californian and Australian Chardonnay, Sauvignon, Chenin Blanc, top-quality white Burgundy, Barsac, Loupiac, good German wines up to Auslese quality, Provence white and rosé, Lirac and Tavel rosé, Loire Cabernet, Alsace, Pinot Noir, Champagne, Cava, dry sherry.

Food	Wine
Red meat courses without too much flavouring or spice	Beaujolais Crus, Rosé, Claret, Burgundy, Rhône, Rioja, lighter Californian and Australian Cabernet Sauvignon, Zinfandel or Shiraz, Italian reds, and just about anything else red you can think of.
Highly spiced or flavoured red meats	Top-quality youngish Claret, top-quality Rhône, heavy Rioja, heavy Italian reds like Tignanello, Californian and Australian Cabernet, Sauvignon, Zinfandel and Shiraz, Provence red, Fitou, Corbières, Cahors.
Spicy oriental cooking (Chinese, Malay, Indian)	Alsace (especially Gewürztraminer), more powerful dry white Loires (good Sancerre, Pouilly Fumé), good dry Rosé, Champagne or Cava, Provence white, red; heavy Rhônes.
Desserts (the trick is to ensure the wine is sweeter than the pudding or it will taste dry)	Muscat de Beaumes de Venise, Sauternes, Barsac, Loupiac, Vouvray (sweet), Champagne, Cava, German wines from Kabinett to Trockenbeerenauslese.

If you're Winewise you'll soon discover which combinations of food and wine you like and which you don't – which foods overpower which wines and so on. Experimenting and trying as many different wines as possible is what makes drinking so much fun! The more you experiment, the more Winewise you become!

Chapter 16

Get Mega-Winewise!

There are several Winewise ways you can find out more about wine without spending a fortune. It's a fun idea to join or form a tasting group. If ten people all bring one bottle, it's a very Winewise way of getting to taste ten wines for the price of one bottle. The Wine Development Board, 5 Kings House, Kennet Wharf Lane, Upper Thames Street, London EC4V 3BH (tel: 01-248 5835), has compiled a list of tasting clubs throughout the country, and several adult education centres run wine appreciation courses. Or you can form your own. You'll find that many wine merchants will be willing to come and give talks and tastings for the group and often they'll do it for free.

Or you can attend merchants' tastings. The best in London are run by La Vigneronne, 105 Old Brompton Road, London SW7 (tel: 01-589 6113) where, for less than the price of a good bottle, you'll get a tutored tasting of around ten wines. Other London merchants who hold regular customer tastings are Bibendum, 113 Regent's Park Road, London NW1 (tel: 01-586 9761); Alex Findlater, 77 Abbey Road, London NW8 (tel: 01-624 7311); Ostlers, 63a Clerkenwell Road, London EC1 (tel: 01-250 1522), particularly good on New World tastings and La Réserve, 65 Walton Street, London SW3 (tel: 01-589 2020). Or try going to some tastings with a very sensible name – Winewise – run by Michael Schuster, 107 Culford Road, London N1 (tel: 01-254 9734).

But don't worry if you're not in London; there are plenty of tastings going on around the country. Buy a copy of *Wine* magazine (tel: 01-891 6070) or *Decanter* magazine (tel: 01-350 1551), available from newsagents and wine shops, and browse through the extensive *Diary* pages, which detail all

sorts of tastings, dinners and wine-related events and
holidays.

Or join a wine club run by a wine company, such as Le
Nez Rouge, 12 Brewery Road, London N7 (tel: 01-609 4711),
Les Amis du Vin, 7 Ariel Way, London W12 (tel:01-740
0053) or The Wine Society (owned by its members), Gunnels
Wood Road, Stevenage, Herts (tel: 0438-314161), who have
discounts for club members and many special events.

Or you can sign up for the Wine and Spirit Education
Trust courses, 5 Kings House, Kennet Wharf Lane, Upper
Thames Street, London EC4V 3BH (which are held in the
evenings and combine practical and tasting knowledge).

It's worth going to good wine bars where you get interesting wines without being ripped off. The best for both food,
wine and atmosphere (not peace and quiet though, because
they're always packed) in London are without a doubt those
owned by New Zealander Don Hewitson: The Cork and
Bottle, 46 Cranbourne Street, London WC2; Shampers, 4
Kingly Street, London W1 and Methuselah's, 92 Victoria
Street, London SW1. The chain of Davy's wine bars, mainly
found in the City, are a good bet, too. The best I've been to
out of London was The Epworth Tap in Epworth, Yorkshire,
well off the beaten track but well worth the detour.

For the best wine bars each year, get hold of a copy of the
Which? Wine Guide (Consumers' Association), available in
libraries, which details the best bars around the country
and includes a list of restaurants where you can take your
own wine. Even if they charge you corkage (a nominal fee
for each bottle opened), this is often a much more Winewise
way of drinking good wines, as you avoid the restaurant
mark-up.

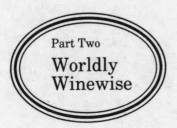

Part Two
Worldly
Winewise

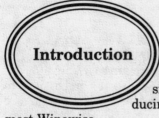

Introduction

This section of *Winewise* explains the best countries and regions to look out for. It's not a comprehensive list of every single wine-producing country in the world, just the most Winewise.

Hopefully by the end of Part Two you'll be Worldly Winewise and nothing will be able to stop you in your Winewise quest!

Chapter 17

The French Connection France is very Winewise – especially if you know where to look. There are so many different styles of wines, it's impossible to get bored. And new Appellations are being created all the time to add to the choice.

Champagne – Bubble Bonanza

Britain is bubbly's biggest boozing nation according to the latest export figures from Champagne, and I'm all for it! Champagne is definitely good for you. Even before my father joined the wine trade, a bottle of Champagne was the only way to celebrate great occasions in our household. My mother first tasted Champagne on her wedding day and decided there could be no other celebration drink. Those who know her well are convinced that's why she had nine children!

Champagne did not exactly flow: it was only served on high days and holidays, weddings, special birthdays and christenings. At the latter the baby generally got a double dose of Champagne, first sucked from a finger dipped in the glass and the second slightly diluted by mother's milk! We were blissfully unaware of the intricacies involved in its making, but a spell spent working in Champagne when I was eighteen saw to that. I had great fun traipsing round the miles and miles of cellars which criss-cross underground beneath the city of Reims, the capital of the Champagne region, explaining to visitors how Champagne was made. The tasting at the end of every visit was not at all hard work – learning to be Winewise about Champagne was very enjoyable! It was also an education, not only in learning to speak French but also in how to consume vast amounts of bubbly and survive!

In the last five years the pattern of Champagne consumption has changed. It's no longer just the racehorse owners, the racing drivers, the stars of stage and screen and the ship-launching set (what a waste!) who are popping the corks. Nor is it just the Sloanes or the Yuppies. Everyone seems to be drinking it. We're lucky to have benefited from a series of good vintages and a price reduction about two years ago, which has transformed it into a much more popular drink. And it was the supermarkets that really whetted our appetite by launching their own-label brands, undercutting the established Grands Marques (well-known names such as Bollinger, Veuve-Clicquot etc.) and bringing Champagne to the supermarket shelves at an affordable price.

But why does Champagne have this cachet? Is it simply a clever marketing gimmick, or is it that it appeals to the traditional British snob value? Producers will tell you avidly that Champagne is unique, because the real stuff can only come from an area of the same name in the north of France. They point out that the special chalk geology, the blend of grapes used and the particular microclimate (not to mention the time-consuming *méthode champenoise* process) all give a distinctive taste which is unique. I think it's rather a combination of all these factors for, however hard I've tried, I've never found another sparkling wine that tastes as good as Champagne.

The Champagne producers, ever jealous of their 'unique' product, have gone to amazing lengths to protect their name. Not only is the term Champagne restricted to the real McCoy on any bottles sold within the Common Market, but from the year 1990 even the term *méthode champenoise* will not be allowed to appear (on any label apart from Champagne), even though it's now an accepted wine-making term. The Champagne producers even stopped the confectionery makers calling Crunchie 'the Champagne bar' – perhaps this was taking trade mark protection just a little too far.

Most Champagne is a blend of three grapes: one white grape, Chardonnay, and two black grapes, Pinot Noir and Pinot Meunier, a fact which still amazes people. There's a simple explanation for this: a grape's skin gives the wine the colour. So in Champagne-making, the grapes are crushed relatively quickly and the juice-staining skins removed. The flesh inside the black grapes is actually whitish, not black as most people expect.

One of the special things about Champagne in wine-making terms is that it is one of the few wines to undergo two fermentations. The first takes place in huge stainless steel vats where the natural sugar in the grape juice transforms into carbon dioxide and alcohol. So that these tanks do not explode, the carbon dioxide is released by way of a valve. After this first fermentation the resulting wine is still.

Then the wine is put into bottles with the addition of yeast. The bottles are taken down to the miles of cellars and left there at a constant temperature for at least two years. The yeast starts to ferment, again creating carbon dioxide and hey presto, you've got bubbly. But then there's a problem. Once the yeast has done its job, it dies, and dead particles float around the wine. Nothing wrong with dead yeast, you might say, but we consumers are very fussy. So a very lengthy process (partially why Champagne will never be cheap) then ensues whereby the dead yeast particles are removed from the bubbly.

The traditional method of doing this is called *remuage* and involves putting all the bottles neck down in a rack called a *pupitre*. Then the bottles are twisted an eighth of a turn each day until they are virtually vertical and all the dead yeast has collected in the neck of the bottle. Skilled *remuagers* can turn as many as 40,000 bottles per day. While interesting for the tourists to watch, this process is time-consuming and expensive. Now most of the major Champagne houses have invested in machinery to do the job: huge computer-operated wire baskets that hold thousands of bottles are tilted to a certain angle day and night. These are much faster than *remuage* by hand, take up less space and don't go on strike!

Then comes the tricky process of getting rid of the sediment without wasting too much of the expensive bubbly.

The bottles are plunged neck first into an ice-cold bath which freezes the Champagne and dead yeast in the neck of the bottle. At this time the bottle has a crown cap similar to a beer bottle lid rather than a cork. This is pulled off and the ice bung containing the dead yeast shoots out of the bottle. This process, known as *dégorgement*, is an impressive operation to watch; the noise of opening bottles is quite deafening. While generally carried out by a machine, the larger bottles are still degorged by hand, and onlooking visitors (or their guide) regularly get soaked with a spray of Champagne.

Then the bottles are topped up with some of the same Champagne and an addition of cane sugar and old Champagne – known as the *dosage*. If a demi-sec Champagne is being made more sugar will be added, but most champagne sold is 'brut' and relatively dry.

In a nutshell the process is time-consuming, but even more care goes into what is called the *assemblage*. If the wine is to be a non-vintage, wines from several different years are blended, as the whole *raison d'être* of a non-vintage wine is that it should have a consistent taste from year to year. Blending is the real skill in Champagne-making, and you can always rely on good non-vintage Champagne from the best Champagne houses. These include: Heidsieck Monopole, Krug, Veuve-Clicquot, Roederer, Piper Heidsieck and Pol Roger.

A vintage wine can be more variable as it is the produce of one year, and therefore will have the special characteristics of that year rather than a house style. So for this reason some produce lighter, elegant wines, others big, rich, round wines and, unless you know the style of a particular vintage, you could be disappointed.

While there are lots of good vintage Champagnes around, it's often more Winewise to go for a non-vintage. I don't think the extra you pay for a vintage is often worthwhile unless it is at least fifteen years old. If you like a less aggressively sharp Champagne but don't want to shell out lots of loot for an expensive vintage, try buying your favourite non-vintage and keeping it for a year or two. It's bound to improve, but remember to write the date you bought it on the case or label!

'Deluxe' Champagnes are there for those with a lot of money to spend. They are generally a vintage (Krug's Grand Cuvée is the exception) and the top of the producer's range. But they tend to be at least double the price of the straight non-vintage, so it's got to be a very special occasion to warrant paying for one bottle of deluxe when you could have two bottles of non-vintage.

There are a few misunderstood words that appear on Champagne labels, the most common being Blanc de Blancs. This simply means the wine has been made entirely from white grapes, the Chardonnay in the case of Champagne. But in general, those made from the traditional blend seem to be my favourites. Don't write off the supermarket and wine merchant's own-label wines until you have tried them. In several recent blind tastings they've come out well and in some cases are actually better than some of the well-known names.

Rosé Champagne seems to be in vogue at the moment and again the leading supermarkets have excellent, competitively priced examples. Traditionally, rosé was made by leaving the black grapes' skins in contact with the juice. But this method proved very difficult to control, as it was easy to end up with too much colour in the wine. Now red wine (from the Champagne region) is normally added to the wine before the second fermentation. Rosé Champagne often has a more fruity taste than the white with more raspberry, earthy flavour from the Pinot Noir (see Chapter 6, 'Grape Expectations').

When do you drink Champagne? Whenever you like! There are lots of ridiculous rules about when it should and should not be drunk, but I love it and don't mind when I drink it! And those people that say it should not be drunk with pudding are wrong. Others say no wine goes with asparagus. That's wrong too. The first meal I had when I met my husband was Krug and asparagus. He supplied the asparagus and I a cherished bottle of Krug. He did better that time, but I've since made up for it!

I don't really believe in using real Champagne for bucks fizz or kir royale – sparkling wine will do. If you're drinking the real thing, it's best to enjoy the taste. There's nothing nicer than the pop of a Champagne bottle, but I prefer to catch what shoots out of the bottle rather than spraying the onlookers racing driver-style. The trick is to make sure the

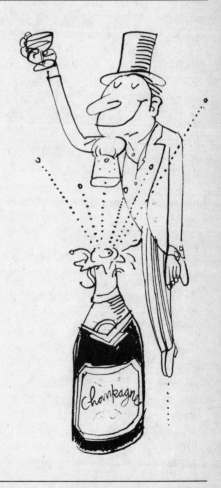

bottle isn't too warm and has not been shaken up. Take off the wire and with your thumb on the top of the cork turn the bottle (not the cork!). All this might sound a bit precious, but it's amazing the number of people who make a hash of opening Champagne bottles, especially wine waiters in restaurants, where you're already paying over the odds so you'd prefer to get it all in your glass!

The Loire – The Vin Valley of France

One of France's most northerly wine-producing regions, the Loire produces lots of dry whites. One of the most widely planted grape varieties is the Chenin Blanc, probably one of the most versatile white grapes in the world as it can naturally produce both dry and sweet wines.

But the wine that has made the Loire Valley known in England is Muscadet, a crisp dry white, and every shop and restaurant will have an example. It varies enormously in quality (the cheapest are often revolting) and it's Winewise to pay a bit more. It's made from a grape of the same name and became popular in France when more people started drinking wine and could not afford the price of white Burgundy. It's a wine made in vast quantities and gulped down without too much fuss.

Apart from basic AC Muscadet, there is another Appellation known as Muscadet de Sèvre-et-Maine, which comes from a smaller region, supposedly of better quality. The most expensive Muscadet, and generally the most interesting, from this region is called Muscadet-sur-Lie. This refers to the way the wine is made. While fermenting it is left on its lees, the natural deposit of dead yeast produced during fermentation. This gives the wine more body and character and a yeasty bouquet. Because it is left untouched during fermentation (in normal wine-making the wine is drained off the lees), natural carbon dioxide is produced which gives the wine a slight spritz (sparkle) which again makes it more interesting as the bubbles seem to project the taste.

Muscadet is at its best when drunk young, so if you're ordering it in a restaurant, check that it's a recent vintage as Muscadet more than two or three years old tends to become rather tired and dull.

Be prepared to pay an extra 50p for a domaine-bottled Muscadet – the quality is worth the extra. While it's unlikely to be the most exciting wine you've ever drunk, it's a good everyday dry white.

There's another wine made in vast quantities in the same region, but which is less well-known in this country. It's called Gros Plant (which refers to the name of the grape used) and is crisp, dry and very high in acidity. It's cheaper

than Muscadet because it does not have Appellation Contrô-lée status – instead it is a VDQS wine. It's a good Winewise buy to go with oily foods, as the high acidity cuts through the food. What's more interesting, though, is that because it is less well-known, it's cheaper than Muscadet. Look out for it in the shops and be Winewise enough to give it a go!

There are plenty of more exciting wines made in the Loire Valley that many people know little about. If you prefer a wine with more character than Muscadet, try Vouvray. This is made from the Chenin Blanc grape, which has a distinctive earthy flavour (see Chapter 6, 'Grape Expectations', for more of its characteristics). It's a grape best drunk young when it is crisp and fresh or left to mature for a few years when it develops a rich, oily, honeyed character. Middle-aged Chenin has a fusty, tired smell.

It's a rich wine even when dry, a wine that is best tasted with food. The sweeter styles will have the words *demi-sec* or *moelleux* on the label and are rich, golden and honeyed, rather like Sauternes. Sparkling Vouvray is delicious, again with the earthy character of the Chenin Blanc grape. It has a very different flavour to Champagne. It's the kind of fizz that people who like definite tastes will enjoy. Good producers include Poniatowski and Huet.

Another good-value Loire bubbly is sparkling Saumur. Like Vouvray, this is made by the time-consuming *méthode champenoise*, again from the Chenin Blanc grape. Saumur tends to be less earthy and rich than Vouvray and should be drunk young, otherwise it loses its freshness.

Sancerre is another well-known name that comes from the central Loire Valley. It suffers from the same over-exposure as Chablis – everyone knows the name and therefore restaurants and shops can sell it at any price. Sancerre is made from the crisp, green, grassy, nettley, gooseberry-flavoured Sauvignon Blanc grape. It's a crisp dry wine with quite a bit of character. It seems to have taken over in popularity from Pouilly Fumé, which is made close by and which was at one time more expensive than Sancerre. It comes from the village and surrounding vineyards of Pouilly Fumé. The name refers to its smoked aroma, often described as gun flint.

But the Winewise among you will go for a less popular wine made from the same grape variety, in a nearby region such as Quincy (yes the same spelling as the detective, although pronounced Can-see), which is generally cheaper and with a similar smoky flinty flavour to Pouilly Fumé. If you see it on a wine list, it should be better value than Sancerre.

Along the same lines, look out for Reuilly and Ménétou-Salon, both made close by to Sancerre and from the same grape. Ménétou-Salon is one of my favourites and is now included on many restaurants' wine lists. Whilst crisp, flinty and dry, it has more body and weight and an aroma of chocolate. As with Muscadet, drink these wines while they're young, which is when the Sauvignon grape is at its most zippy.

With vintages in the Loire, you can follow the general rule that years with hot summers will produce wines with less mouth-puckering acidity, a characteristic of both the northerly situation of the Loire and years without much sunshine.

There are plenty of good value Vins de Pays wines from the Loire which have the vague words 'Jardin de la France' on the label. From Touraine look out for wines made from Gamay, the fruity Beaujolais grape.

Bigger, more powerful reds can also be found in the Loire. These come from three areas: Chinon, Bourgueil and Saumur-Champigny. They are made from the grassy Cabernet Franc grape, which is stalky and astringent when young but which ages well. These wines have a distinctive taste and frequently offer better value than their similarly priced claret counterparts. Look out for them on restaurant lists, especially older vintages.

Burgundy – Untangle the Confusion

How does Burgundy relate to Winewise readers? At first glance Burgundy doesn't seem at all Winewise. After all, whenever anyone mentions Burgundy, most people think, 'expensive'. Sadly, there's a lot of truth there, but on the bright side there are plenty of younger growers making fantastic, mouth-watering wines, often from areas which the traditional Burgundy drinker has never heard of.

Burgundy makes both red and white wines. There are two major grapes grown, the white Chardonnay and the red Pinot Noir (see Chapter 6, 'Grape Expectations'). The styles and characteristics of these grapes grown in Burgundy are aspired to worldwide. But hard as they try, Burgundy's distinctive character cannot really be imitated, so it is well worth getting right back to the roots.

It's important to be Winewise about Burgundy – there's major rip-off potential – and getting to grips with the region requires some superhuman Winewise strength. It's important to know some of the lesser-known names that represent the best value for money. For the time being forget the Gevrey-Chambertins and Nuits St Georges, as the names alone don't guarantee great quality. The key is to remember the producer's name, often more important than the name of the vineyard itself. Look for the alternative regions that are the real Winewise bargain Burgundies.

Many people say 'Burgundy isn't what it used to be', and they're right. Because Burgundy is one of the most northerly French vineyards, it receives less sunlight, and therefore it's more difficult to produce fully ripened grapes, high in sugar and potential alcohol. Because of this, it used to be standard practice to blend in powerful, more alcoholic, wines from the Rhône Valley to the south. This was not illegal until the Appellation laws were tightened up in 1972 and Rhône wine was disallowed – from then on Burgundy was going to be pure, despite what it tasted like. It took producers a long time to come to terms with this change in the law (and some still haven't), so the reputation of Burgundy over the last ten years has been far from Wine-

wise. In the seventies, every time there was a poor vintage,
thin, light wines were the result – no wonder Burgundy got
a bad name. But now many producers, especially the
younger ones who have taken most opportunity of the
technical advances of the last fifteen years, are making
authentic wines of a consistent quality – and they can be a
really Winewise choice.

Burgundy is totally different to that other famous French
region, Bordeaux. The main reason why it is so complicated
is that within one vineyard there are sometimes as many as
a hundred owners. In Bordeaux there would be only one
owner for the same, if not larger, area. So the variations
between the styles of several bottles, all carrying the same
vineyard name on the label, can be immense.

It's back to the basic Winewise advice – the name of the
producer is more important than the name of the vineyard.
If you find a producer whose wines you like, make a note of
his name and try some of his other wines, because you'll
probably like them too.

There are two types of producer in Burgundy: the *négo-
ciant* and the grower. The former buys in wines from
different properties and blends them, and the latter will
often make a more characterful wine. This is where eagle-
eyed label-reading can come in handy. In general, wines
from growers rather than *négociants* are more individual;
the former make standard-quality wines, but for the real
excitement look for the words *propriétaire-récoltant* or *mis
en bouteille au domaine* on the label.

Today it's a growing trend for growers to bottle and sell
their own wines rather than selling to the *négociants* who
blend to make standard, reliable wines but which often lack
the edge. But there are good reliable *négociants*, including
Louis Jadot, Louis Latour, Joseph Drouhin, Charles Viénot,
Bouchard Père et Fils, and Remoissenet Père et Fils.

Generally, if you find a grower's Burgundy in Britain, it
shows that the grower has taken the trouble to stand on his
own two feet and that a merchant in England has thought
the quality sufficiently high to import it. Grower-Burgun-
dies are not cheap, and therefore haven't just been bought
for their competitive price.

Bourgogne Blanc and Rouge are like the building blocks of Burgundy without the finished house, in that they can be mini-examples of the amazing wines the Chardonnay and Pinot Noir grapes can produce without the lingering complexity. To begin your Winewise exploration of Burgundy, it's not a bad idea to start with the basics. Bourgogne Blanc and Rouge are not from one specific area, but can be a blend of wines from all over the general region. You can depend upon them if they are from a good producer. If he's any good, he will ensure that his cheapest wine is of a decent quality – otherwise what incentive do potential punters have to buy his higher quality wines? Often the best producers will down-grade some of their wines to Bourgogne Blanc or Rouge if they don't think the quality is up to scratch. For example, a grower in Meursault might down-grade some barrels of Meursault to Bourgogne Blanc if they are not good enough to go into the *Grand Vin* or are made from younger wines.

Bourgogne Rouge will give you the basic flavour of the Pinot Noir, a soft raspberry, earthy-tasting wine. Bourgogne Blanc is rich and ripe with a clean citrus tang. Both are quick-maturing and generally enjoyed best when young.

Some of the individual growers may not produce basic Bourgogne Blanc and Rouge; if they don't, try their cheapest wines and apply the same principle. And if you find a wine you really like, remember the grower's name and experiment with some of his other wines.

Geographically, Burgundy stretches from Chablis in the north to Beaujolais (see the next section, 'Beaujolais') in the south. The central area is the Côte d'Or, consisting of the Côte de Nuits in the north and the Côte de Beaune in the south. Further south is the Côte Chalonnaise, then the Côte Mâconnais, then Beaujolais.

Chablis Chablis is not a very Winewise region. Its wines can be delicious – dry, buttery whites – but they are very expensive. Near Chablis is a small area called St Bris. Here, unlike the rest of Burgundy where the white Chardonnay grape reigns supreme, the Sauvignon grape is grown. Good

Sauvignon de St Bris is delicious, with a gooseberry/choco-
latey nose and rich dry fruit – it's a lot cheaper than Chablis
and those that find their way to Britain can be more
enjoyable than a cheap Chablis. Which is not to say there
aren't any good Chablis to be found – there are – but there
tend to be a lot of dull ones around too.

Styles in the Chablis region include: Dry white, light-
weight: Bourgogne Blanc, Bourgogne Aligoté; dry white,
medium-weight: Chablis, Sauvignon de St Bris. Good producers: Fèvre, La Chablisienne, Pic, Louis Michel, Lamblin,
Long-Depaquit, Servin, Durup and Raveneau.

Côte de Nuits The Côte de Nuits, producing mainly red
wine, is not generally a very Winewise region, because the
wines are so expensive. But to help the Winewise reader
with a deep pocket, here's a guide to styles and particularly
good producers! Wines which won't break the bank include
Côte-de-Nuits Villages, Fixin, Bourgogne Rouge and Blanc.

Red, medium- to heavy-weight: Gevrey-Chambertin,
Chambolle-Musigny, Vougeot, Nuits St Georges, Vosne-
Romanée, Fixin; red, light- to medium-weight: Côte-de-
Nuits Villages, Bourgogne Rouge; white, light- to medium-
weight: Nuits St Georges, Fixin, Bourgogne Blanc. Good
producers: Domaine de la Romanée Conti, Leroy, Dujac,
Drouhin-Larose, Belin, Rousseau, Rion, Trapet, Michelot,
Roty, Clerget and Jayer.

Côte de Beaune Côte de Beaune reds are more earthy than
the wines of the Côte de Nuits. Again, they are not particularly Winewise because of their prices although, as they are
less fashionable than the Côte de Nuits, they can be worth
investigating. For example, red Chassagne, grown on similar soil to the Côte de Nuits and much overshadowed by its
famous white counterpart, is often good value on a wine list.
Other reds like St Aubin, St Romain, Savigny-les-Beaune,
Beaune, Pernand-Vergelesses, Auxey-Duresses, Volnay and
Pommard can also be worth seeking out.

And the Côte de Beaune is where all those whites come

from. Of the famous names, the best value can often be found in Chassagne-Montrachet or Meursault (sometimes better value than Pouilly Fuissé), and lesser-known whites like Savigny, Auxey-Duresses, St Romain, St Aubin or Pernand-Vergelesses can offer excellent value.

Red, medium- to heavy-weight: Aloxe-Corton, Corton, Pernand-Vergelesses, Chorey-les-Beaune, Pommard, Volnay, Meursault, Auxey-Duresses, Chassagne-Montrachet; red, light- to medium-weight: Savigny-les-Beaune, Beaune, Puligny-Montrachet, Santenay, Côte de Beaune Villages, Saint Aubin, Saint Romain.

White, dry, medium- to heavy-weight: Pernand-Vergelesses, Puligny-Montrachet, Chassagne-Montrachet, Meursault; white, dry, light- to medium-weight: Santenay, Saint Romain, Savigny, Bourgogne Blanc. Good producers: Jean Gros, Roumier, Lafon, Girard-Vollot, Bize, Dubreuil-Fontaine, P. Morey, A. Morey, Millot-Battault, Blagn-Gagnard, Michelot, Marchard de Gramant, Tollot-Beaut, Roumier, Clerget, Leflaive, Sauzet, Niellon, Matrot, Clair-Dau, Clerc, Gras, Chandon de Briailles.

Côte Chalonnaise The Côte Chalonnaise is very Winewise – offering reds and whites made from the Pinot Noir and Chardonnay at a fraction of the price of the Côte d'Or. The main names to watch out for are Rully, Givry, Mercurey and Montagny. They never show the wonderful sophistication of the best Côte d'Or wines, but there are many sub-standard wines from the Côte d'Or selling at high prices because of their name that are put to shame by many Côte Chalonnaise wines.

Red and white, dry, light- to medium-weight: Rully, Mercurey, Givry, Montagny. Good producers: Domaine de la Renarde (André Delorme), Villaine, Cogny, Bernard Michel.

Mâconnais The Mâcon district is made up of lots of villages, most of which call themselves Mâcon-something. There are a few exceptions like Pouilly-Fuissé, Pouilly-Vinzelles and

St Véran, more of which later. It can be a Winewise region,
provided you buy from the right producer (rather like the
Côte d'Or but a lot cheaper). The wines are almost always
white, dry and medium to medium- to light-bodied. They're
made from the same grape as the Côte d'Or whites, the
Chardonnay.

Always try to buy a village wine in preference to a generic
wine (i.e. Mâcon-Viré instead of plain Mâcon). Pouilly-
Fuissé, arguably one of the best wines of the area, has now
reached such a price level that it's definitely not a Winewise
buy. But neighbouring Pouilly-Vinzelles and St Véran are
still excellent value.

White, dry, light-weight: Mâcon-Villages, Mâcon, Mâcon-
Viré, Mâcon-Lugny, Mâcon-Prissé, Mâcon-Clessé, Mâcon-
Loché; White, dry, medium-weight: Saint Véran, Pouilly-
Vinzelles, Mâcon-Fuissé, Mâcon-Vinzelles, Pouilly-Fuissé.
Good producers: Duboeuf, Loron, Cave Coop, Vincent, Las-
serat, Lucquet, Bon Gran. Red, light-weight: Mâcon Rouge.

Beaujolais – Not Just the Nouveau Way

'Beau jolly', as it is often pronounced by imbibing Yuppies, is not a bad description. For this is a Winewise fun wine which can be amazing value for money. Beaujolais Nouveau was, and still is to some extent, the marketing success of the 1960s. Up until that time it had existed very much as Burgundy's poor relation. But the razzmatazz of Nouveau, the race to see who could get the first bottles back to England by car, Roller or parachute (well, aeroplane as well), all combined to make Beaujolais Nouveau front-page news. Producers who used to have to wait until at least the following summer for their money rubbed their hands in glee. And you have to hand it to the marketing men, they certainly did a good job. People who don't buy a bottle of wine all year long often splash out on a bottle of Nouveau.

Producers in the Beaujolais region were delighted. In fact, Beaujolais Nouveau has become such big business around the world that it currently accounts for more than half of all the wine produced in Beaujolais.

A few other areas such as Muscadet and Bordeaux have attempted to jump on the Nouveau bandwagon, without anything like as much success. It's the characteristics of the Gamay grape and the method of vinification which make Beaujolais suitable for drinking early. The Gamay is a very fruity grape (See Chapter 6, 'Grape Expectations') and the way it is made (*macération carbonique* – see Chapter 5, 'Converting the Grapes'), results in a wine which has lots of bubblegum-flavoured fruit and a low tannin level.

But when it comes to smooth drinking, Nouveau doesn't get a look-in. The poor grapes barely have a chance to ripen before they are whisked off the vines and plunged into the bottle. It's a small wonder that whole bunches of grapes don't fall out of Nouveau bottles! By the time the last bottle of Nouveau has left the shops, it is just about becoming pleasant to drink. Beaujolais Nouveau drunk after Christmas is always much more enjoyable than when it's first released. But most people think it is definitely untrendy to serve Nouveau more than a few weeks after its release date. They are not Winewise!

In any case, any Nouveau that is not sold or has stayed with the maker can perfectly legitimately be re-labelled straight Beaujolais (as it is exactly the same wine), and people will then order it quite happily in a restaurant. So if you see any Nouveau being sold off cheaply, go for it. It might have some sediment in the bottom of the bottle, but it should taste delicious.

Apart from the straight Beaujolais, you can find Beaujolais Villages, a slightly higher-quality level which has to come from certain designated villages. Occasionally some shops offer a Villages Nouveau, which is generally a little more expensive, but probably worth it.

Beaujolais Crus (separately named Villages) are often the bargains of the wine list, as restaurants generally sell more Beaujolais in the two weeks of Nouveau than they do during the rest of the year. As a result they are left with the superior wines. This is where the Winewise reader steps in to help out!

Although there are thirty-nine villages which are entitled to the Appellation Beaujolais Villages, there are only nine which may use their own name. These Grand Cru Beaujolais are of a much higher quality as the yields are restricted and the wine is generally made with much more care than Nouveau. And it cannot be released for sale until almost a month after Nouveau.

These wines can be kept for a few years and the best vintages even longer. They have much more depth of flavour than Nouveau, and are far more interesting wines. What's more, they all have easy-to-remember names.

St Amour is one of the lighter Crus, aromatic, elegant, the wine we love to drink. As a result of its romantic name, it is much in demand and sometimes difficult to find.

The vineyards of Chiroubles have the highest elevation in the Beaujolais hills and, probably because of the distinctly French-sounding name, the wine has never really been much in evidence in Britain. It's the *chic* wine to drink in Paris wine bars and is one of the lighter Crus, generally drunk by the French before the Easter following the harvest. After that it can lack the intense fruity flavour of some of the other Crus.

Chénas is the smallest of the Crus, and takes its name from the old oak trees which used to grow in the village. Ironically, though, these trees which made the wine famous have now been cut down to make way for more vines. This is a relatively full-bodied style of wine found on the more innovative lists.

Sales of Morgon (not the car but the wine; the wine came first!) have accelerated faster than other Beaujolais, perhaps because of its desirable name. Wouldn't you like to own a Morgon? But because it's such a big area, not all producers seem to have got into gear and it's not all of the same calibre. Often its aroma is likened to cherries or kirsch.

Brouilly has become quite popular in Britain and is in the heart of the Beaujolais region. Whilst elegant, it has good rich flavour and its neighbour Côte de Brouilly (another Cru) is even fuller, often with a higher alcohol content.

Juliénas (no, not a way of cutting vegetables!) is a tasty wine. It ages well, is well-structured and powerful.

Fleurie, easy to pronounce and even easier to drink, is a best-seller in Britain. Sexist wine tasters (or writers) will give it a female gender, describing it as feminine and fragrant, characteristics which have earned the wine the title 'Queen of Beaujolais' (using the regal sense of the word).

But where there is a queen, story books tell us that there has to be a king. Moulin-à-Vent (ever heard of a wine named after a windmill?) takes the crown as the 'King of Beaujolais', and is supposedly the longest-lasting Beaujolais Cru. It's the most powerful, and older vintages taste much more like Pinot Noir from the Côte d'Or than Gamay.

So next time someone asks you to order 'Beau Jolly', go the whole Cru, because you are Winewise!

Bordeaux – Without Paying the Dough

You've heard of the bottle of wine selling for £100,000 at auction, and you're sure it couldn't have been a Winewise reader who bought it! You'd probably be right, but it's likely that it was a claret from Bordeaux, the region that produces some of the most famous (and expensive) wines in the world.

But Winewise readers are looking for Bordeaux wines without paying that kind of dough. And there's plenty that's good value if you know where to look. But you need to be aware of the red herrings you'll encounter along the way, wines that have famous-sounding names but aren't quite the same thing, and wines where you're simply paying for the name. A château can be anything from a very grand property among the vines to a little shack. And don't think that the bigger the château the better the wine – it doesn't work like that.

Bordeaux produces mostly red wines, although there are some dry whites (Graves and Entre-Deux-Mers) and a number of sweet wines (Sauternes, Barsac, Loupiac, Monbazillac).

Unlike some other French regions, and most Californian and Australian wines, Bordeaux has never put the grape variety on the label. To the Winewise reader this might seem rather silly, but there is a very good reason: the red wines are made from a blend of up to five different grape varieties: Cabernet Sauvignon, Merlot (the main ones), Petit Verdot, Malbec and Cabernet Franc. The first two generally make up most of the blend: Cabernet Sauvignon in the Médoc and Graves, Merlot in St Emilion, Pomerol and Entre-Deux-Mers. It's a good idea for the Winewise reader to remember these regions – the Cabernet Sauvignon produces hard, tannic, blackcurranty wines and the Merlot softer, rounder wines. So a Médoc wine will be more tannic when it is the same age as a St Emilion wine, and so best if kept a bit longer.

There are hundreds of different Bordeaux wines available in Britain, and apart from recognising the characteristic high-shouldered bottle (see Chapter 1, 'Bottle Bulge'), there are plenty of other signs on the label to help you make your choice.

The table below will help you be Winewise about Bordeaux with as little pain as possible. It's not comprehensive, but is a basic guide to what's available.

Area name	Style	Main grape variety	Price (£££,££,£)*
RED WINES			
Bordeaux	Mid-weight, fruity, or hard and austere	Cabernet Sauvignon	£
Bordeaux Supérieur	Similar style as Bordeaux, but better quality	Cabernet Sauvignon	£
Entre-Deux-Mers	Soft, rounded	Cabernet Sauvignon/ Merlot	£
St Estèphe	Tannic, needs keeping	Cabernet Sauvignon	££–£££
Pauillac	Tannic, rich fruit	Cabernet Sauvignon	££–£££
St Julien	Less tannic, more elegant	Cabernet Sauvignon	££–£££
Margaux	Supple and rounded	Cabernet Sauvignon/ Merlot	££–£££
Haut-Médoc	Firm, tannic	Cabernet Sauvignon	£–££
Médoc	Similar to Haut-Médoc, but lower quality	Cabernet Sauvignon	£–££
Graves	Mid-weight, fruity	Cabernet Sauvignon	£–££
St Emilion	Soft, rich, velvety	Merlot	£–£££
Pomerol	Similar to St Emilion but more chocolatey, firmer	Merlot	££–£££

Area name	Style	Main grape variety	Price (£££,££,£)*
Fronsac, Canon Fronsac, Côtes de Castillon, Côtes de Francs, St Georges St Emilion, Lussac St Emilion, Montagne St Emilion	Like lesser St Emilions – lightish-weight, fruity, drink young	Cabernet Franc/ Merlot	£–££
Côtes de Bourg et Blaye	Medium-weight, a bit like mini-Médocs	Cabernet Sauvignon	£–££
WHITE WINES			
Entre-Deux-Mers	Fresh dry whites	Sauvignon Blanc/Semillon	£
Graves	Many boring but a few good dry whites	Sauvignon Blanc/Semillon	£–£££
Sauternes and Barsac, Loupiac, Monbazillac	Sweet, rich and luscious	Sauvignon Blanc/Semillon	££–£££
Sainte Croix-du-Mont	Mini-Sauternes	Sauvignon Blanc/Semillon	£–££

*£ – cheap   ££ – medium prices   £££ – expensive

Generic clarets are those wines that just say Bordeaux on the label. Generally a merchant's or supermarket's own label variety (often referred to as house claret) is a better bet than an unknown one. If you find one you like, look for the producer's name and try to remember it. Styles of house claret vary greatly: some are the modern, fruity variety, others the more traditional austere, tannic kind. The only way of knowing is to try the wines and remember the producer's name of ones you like.

Petit Châteaux wines are not those from small châteaux,

rather those from lesser-known properties which were not classified in the famous 1855 classification of Bordeaux châteaux. Often these wines represent good value for

money. Many will have the words 'Bordeaux Supérieur' on the label, a higher-quality level than straight Bordeaux. In addition the Entre-Deux-Mers area, generally known for its white wines, is making some good fruity reds which are very reasonably priced. But watch out – just because there's a château name on the label, there's no guarantee that the wine will be good.

Médoc wines with the words 'Grand Cru Classé' are the top wines of Bordeaux and as a result the most expensive. The majority need keeping for several years until they are ready for drinking unless they are from a light or less good vintage. They are classified into Crus (or growths) where the first growths are the best quality (names like Lafite, Latour), going down to fifth growths. But since this classification was made way back in 1855, you need to watch out – some fifth growths can be as good as second growths. It's all an evil plot to confuse the wine drinker!

As an indication of their style, look for the names of the commune on the label (eg. Pauillac, Saint Julien). These wines are expensive because they are in such high demand all over the world. But this does not mean that they are unsuitable for the Winewise reader – it depends on his or her budget. They can be the most Winewise of all wines because they are of such superb quality. Even so, there are still some good value wines to be found, relatively undervalued. They include: Châteaux Haut-Batailley, d'Issan, Haut-Bages-Libéral, Kirwan, Langoa-Barton, Léoville-Barton and St Pierre.

Getting in First Winewise claret drinkers ought to take advantage of buying claret *en primeur*. This means buying the wine of a good vintage and paying for it while it is in cask, long before it's even bottled. It might sound odd, but it can be the cheapest way of buying claret. By the time your wine is shipped over to Britain, the market price could well have doubled. By buying early, you benefit from the best possible price – but you need to trust both your merchant's tasting ability – and honesty. Many of the independent merchants listed in Chapter 12, 'Bottle Stop', sell claret *en primeur*.

Go For Bourgeois But amongst the best buys in the Médoc are the Crus Bourgeois. These are wines not classified in 1855, which often offer the Winewise reader the same quality as a classed growth but at a fraction of the price. Ones to look out for include: Chasse-Spleen, Potensac, Monbrison, Meyney, Ormes-de-Pez, Poujeaux, Cissac, La Tour de By, Sociando-Mallet and Tour du Haut Moulin.

A Second Chance The very best châteaux carry out a selection procedure. If they feel a certain vat is not up to scratch, they don't put it into the main wine. Together with wine produced from young vineyards, they make what is called a second wine. This is like a mini-version of the Grand Vin, is faster-maturing and, what's more, is generally less than half the price. While some of them use the château name on the label (like Pavillon Rouge de Château Margaux, the second wine of Château Margaux), others have totally different names, so you need to be Winewise to trace them down. The most commonly found in Britain are real Winewise bargains, in shops and restaurants, and are a way of drinking the style of the world's top wines without paying top prices.

Name of Grand Vin	Second Wine
Château Margaux	Pavillon Rouge de Château Margaux
Château Haut-Brion	Bahans-Haut-Brion
Château Brane Cantenac	Domaine de Fontarney/Ch Notton
Château Montrose	La Dame de Montrose
Château Ducru Beaucaillou	La Croix
Château Gruaud-Larose	Sarget de Gruaud-Larose
Château Léoville Lascases	Clos du Marquis
Château Pichon-Longueville-Lalande	Réserve de la Comtesse
Château Talbot	Connétable de Talbot
Château Grand-Puy-Lacoste	Lacoste-Boire
Château Haut-Bailly	La Parde de Haut-Bailly
Château Prieuré-Lichine	Château de Clairefont

Saint Emilion Here the classification system is a lot more complicated. There are literally hundreds of wines with the words 'Grand Cru' on the label – unfortunately this does not always guarantee quality. Some generic Saint Emilions can be every bit as good. But 'Grand Cru Classé' indicates a better quality wine and often, because many of the wines from Saint Emilion are not as well-known as those of the Médoc, they represent better value.

The very top wines, and therefore the most expensive, are the Premier Grand Cru Classés. But Winewise châteaux in St Emilion which offer both value for money and quality include: Larmande, l'Arrosée, Fombrauge, Cadet Piola, Cap de Mourlin, Pavie-Decesse, Fonroque, Franc Grâce Dieu, Bellevue-Mondotte and l'Angélus.

Pomerol Next to St Emilion is Pomerol. This area includes many small vineyards, a few making some of the world's top wines. These include Petrus, Vieux-Château-Certan, Certan de May, L'Eglise-Clinet, Lafleur, Trotanoy and Le Bon-Pasteur. But they're not cheap, and only the Winewise reader with a well-lined pocket can afford to indulge in them.

As well as the wines of Saint Emilion and Pomerol themselves, there are several surrounding areas that make good value-for-money wines. These include Lalande de Pomerol, Saint-Georges-Saint-Emilion, Côtes de Francs, Fronsac and Lussac.

The Côtes-de-Bourg and Blaye are two regions producing Médoc-style wines which can be very good value because the area is less well known.

The Whites Many basic-quality dry whites come from the Entre-Deux-Mers region. They are generally cheap and (fairly) cheerful, although better quality can be found from wines labelled Bordeaux Sauvignon which are often crisper and more aromatic.

But the best quality whites come from a few properties in the Graves where they are fermenting their wine in new oak barrels – the wines have lots of Sauvignon and Semillon character combined with complexity. Whilst they are not cheap, they can be very Winewise wines as alternatives to more expensive white Burgundies. Names to look out for include (recent vintages only): Domaine de Chevalier, de Fieuzal, Rahoul, Domaine Benoît, Smith-Haut-Lafitte, Malartic-Lagravière, La Tour-Martillac, Reynon, Montalivet and La Louvière.

Although famous for its red wines, Bordeaux also produces one of the world's greatest white wines, Sauternes. This is made from grapes which appear to the untrained eye to be no good for anything because they are rotten. But this special type of so-called 'noble rot' affects the grape skins and, as the grapes shrivel up, their sugar content becomes more concentrated. The resulting wine is rich, luscious, but extremely difficult and costly to produce. Barsac, another name you will see on labels of sweet white, is an area within Sauternes producing similar-style wines.

Mini-Sauternes-style wines which are much cheaper include wines made in the neighbouring regions of Loupiac, Cérons and Sainte Croix-du-Mont, generally good value in shops and wine lists.

South-West France – Beefy Reds

This might sound like an 'also-ran' chapter, but it's one of the most Winewise chapters in the book. Wines from these lesser-known areas are brilliant value for money, for that very reason. Wines that everyone knows the name of are rarely the best value because, as soon as they reach that dizzy height, the price goes up. So a good look at wines from these regions reveals some amazing buys.

South-west France covers many regions. To define it geographically, take the south-west corner of France and exclude Bordeaux. It covers literally hundreds of wines so here I've selected the best ones available in Britain. As a massive generalisation, the reds are dark in colour and have quite a powerful earthy flavour. The hot climate tends to favour the making of sweet whites rather than dry and many of the latter are flat and lacking in acidity. There are lots of good Winewise rosés to be found, much more pleasant and drier than the dumpy-bottled Portuguese variety that sells like hot cakes in Britain.

Search out Vin de Pays wines, especially from the Pyrenees, and don't subscribe to that commonly held misconception that unless it's an Appellation Contrôlée wine it's not worth buying. Look out for some of the following names.

Bergerac Although it shares the same name as the detective, you won't find this wine quite as hard to pin down. Several good supermarkets and independents stock it. The area is situated in the Dordogne, not far from Bordeaux. As a result, the red wines are made from the same grape varieties: Cabernet Sauvignon, Cabernet Franc and Merlot. But their added attraction is that they are fresh and fruity, generally lighter than generic claret, and can be drunk much younger.

There are a few top properties such as Château de la Jaubertie owned by Englishman Henry Ryman. Having established a very successful chain of stationery shops of the same name in Britain, he then sold out in search of an idyllic life in France. Now he has made his château famous and, apart from excellent everyday-drinking red and white wines, he ages his best red wines in wood, which gives them much more body and makes them even more similar to a good Bordeaux wine.

If you're in the region, look out for red Bergeracs with the Côtes de Bergerac AC, which rarely find their way to Britain but can be of a slightly higher quality than basic Bergerac. In addition there's another area within Bergerac that has its own AC, Pécharmant, which often makes some of the fullest wines of the region.

White Bergerac can be dry or sweet and is made from the Sauvignon and Semillon grape. Today most of the white Bergerac which gets as far as Britain is generally dry. Henry Ryman's son, who trained as a winemaker in Australia, is now making excellent wood-aged dry whites which should be available soon. If you see the word *moelleux* on the label that means it's sweet, but watch out, because some Bergeracs can have as much as 15 per cent alcohol.

Buzet A wine with a name like this has just got to be Winewise. Pronounced boozey, this wonderfully named village can be found eighty miles south-east of Bordeaux in the Lot-et-Garronne region. Its full name is Côtes de Buzet, but often wines are labelled simply Buzet. If you visit this area in the summer, you'll be amazed that they make wine because all along the valleys the fields are full of huge sunflowers. But if you take a detour into the hills, you'll find the vines. Most of the wine in this region is made at a huge co-operative, one of the most efficiently run co-ops in France. Buzet is a must for Winewise readers who like claret but don't like the price. It's very similar in style, comes in a claret-shaped bottle (see Chapter 1, 'Bottle Bulge') and even tastes like claret because it's made from the classic Bordeaux grapes, Cabernet Sauvignon, Cabernet Franc and Merlot. But its great advantage is that it can be drunk much younger. It's a smooth, easy-drinking red with masses of blackcurrant-flavoured fruit.

Look out for the co-operative's top wine called Cuvée Napoléon, which has an impressive black and gold label.

And it's not just the label that looks good – the wine is delicious. It's best to be patient and keep it for a few years because it's a big, full red which has been aged in new oak casks and is therefore quite tannic.

Some white and rosé wines are made, but they don't seem to get as far as Britain and are mostly consumed locally; they're worth a try if you're in the area.

Cahors Cahors is a really big blockbuster of a wine and if you're given it blind you can often recognise it by its very deep purple inky colour. It's made much further south than Bergerac and driving south you'll see lots of signposts for the town of Cahors. Unless you enjoy giving your teeth a tannin bath, it's best not to drink Cahors until it's at least a few years old. If you find any really old vintages on restaurant wine lists it's a good bet, as these wines have the structure to last for ages. It's good value for money, although more expensive than other south-western reds. In the region it's drunk with strong dishes such as duck and goes well with very strong pongy cheeses.

Côtes de Duras This area isn't far from Bergerac and its wines are fairly similar. The reds are light and fruity, made from the same grapes as Bergerac, enjoyable to drink when young and the whites are dry and crisp with a high percentage of the zingy Sauvignon grape. You're likely to come across the whites much more often than the reds, because the production is twice as high.

Gaillac If you can remember the name, wines from this area are a good buy because they're very cheap and well made. They're produced in the *département* called Tarn, another name worth remembering, because it produces very good Vins de Pays. On the labels of the dry white wines you might find the word *perlé* which means the wine will be slightly sparkling. They are refreshingly crisp and aromatic, great for a summer's day. And the rosés are not dissimilar, but have an even more powerful aroma. What makes them so enjoyable is that they are dry – there's nothing worse than medium-sweet, sickly rosé.

The reds are light, jammy and very fruity, many now being made by the same *macération carbonique* method used for Beaujolais.

Jurançon No, not the French way of pronouncing that well-known pop group Duran Duran's name, but that's exactly what it sounds like without pronouncing the 'j'. This area is well known for its rich sweet whites, which have the word *moelleux* on the label. Grapes are left on the vines until they are brown and shrivelled and look good for absolutely nothing. But the resulting wine, which is luscious, raisiny and sweet, just proves that seeing isn't believing. However, if you're partial to a drop of Jurançon, you must check the labels carefully, because they also make a dry (*sec*) wine which is less interesting than the Moelleux.

Madiran A powerful red, almost as dark in colour as Cahors. All Madiran has to be aged in wood, so is not generally suitable for drinking very young. The co-operative make a reasonably priced example, and single-grower Madirans can be of excellent quality. Whilst not widely available, they are well worth searching out.

Monbazillac This is a good, much cheaper Winewise alternative to Sauternes. It's made in Dordogne to the south of Bergerac. It's made in the same way as Sauternes and is often even higher in alcohol with rich, luscious, sweet fruit. It's amazingly good value and can be enjoyed young or old.

Côtes du Marmandais The white wines tend to have a rather hot and sticky aroma which can smell like marmalade and reminds me of their name. It's a VDQS area in the Lot-et-Garronne *département* which also makes soft, fruity reds good for everyday drinking at the bottom of the price range.

The Rhône – Valley of the Giants

Winewise readers will soon come to grips with the great wines of the Rhône (in more ways than one, but more of that later!), as this area must be one of the most overlooked areas of France for quality and amazing value for money. The Rhône's top wines can equal the greatest of Bordeaux and Burgundy, but are much cheaper and the quality of the everyday wines is good too. In fact, lots of people in the past unknowingly drank lots of Rhône wines in the days when it was normal to blend it into Burgundy. This practice is now illegal, but if you are lucky enough to drink a good old bottle of pre-1972 Burgundy, you'll probably be drinking some Rhône wine.

But today it has an identity all of its own, and because not all the world realises its potential, it's often a great Winewise buy in wine shops and restaurants. And there's a lot more to it than Côtes-du-Rhône, which is generally a safe bet and rarely disappoints. Its exactly what one would expect from the hot climate of southern France, a ripe jammy wine with what's described as a peppery finish. No, this doesn't mean it tastes of cayenne pepper, rather that it has a hot, slightly spicy taste on the finish.

It's an impressive area to visit if you're ever driving to the south of France. The vineyards are not unlike those of the Duoro Valley in Portugal, with very steep slopes and terraced vineyards. They're the sort of vineyards which make me very glad I've never been on a grape-picking holiday (some holiday!). It's also an area full of really good restaurants. Allow plenty of time to sample the cuisine as well as the wines.

But back in cloudy Britain, what are the best buys from the Rhône? In simple terms, it's easiest to think about the Rhône split into two parts: the north and the south. The north produces the top wines – big, heavy and tannic (that's where the grip comes in) when young, with the ability to age well. Names include Hermitage, Côte Rôtie, Crozes-Hermitage, Cornas and St-Joseph. Côte Rôtie and Cornas make only red wines, and the other three are mainly red,

but also produce very small quantities of white. Look for
vintages of the red wines over five years old – they'll almost
always be great value. There are a number of good producers, some of whom are *négociants* and some growers: Paul
Jaboulet Ainé, Chave, Jasmin, Clape and Guigal.

There are also two areas which produce only top-quality,
if expensive, white wine in tiny quantities: Condrieu and
Château-Grillet. If you want to boggle the minds of your
wine-fanatic friends, produce the odd bottle or two of these –
they'll be impressed! The style is dry but with more oiliness
than, for instance, Muscadet, and they have a high natural
alcohol level resulting from the hot local climate.

Finally from the northern Rhône, there's a really tasty
little fizz, made by the same method as Champagne, called
St Péray. It's not as expensive as Champagne and is well
worth finding. At the moment it's not widely distributed.

But it's the southern Rhône which will really appeal to
Winewise drinkers in search of good value, affordable wines
for everyday drinking. This is the home of Côtes-du-Rhône,
already a deservedly popular wine. Because there are so
many producers in this large area, there are all sorts of
different Côtes-du-Rhône available, and the only way to tell
which one agrees with your taste buds is to put a few to the
tasting test – try not to forget which ones you like! Then
there's Côtes-du-Rhône-Villages – this is of a higher quality
than straight Côtes-du-Rhône, and comes from specific villages in the region.

Additionally, there are various villages which produce
wines in their own right: Gigondas, Vacqueyras, Cairanne,
Rasteau and others. These are fantastic value, provided you
hit lucky with a good winemaker. In the south there are
also three large areas capable of producing good, inexpensive, everyday-drinking wines: Côtes du Ventoux, Coteaux
du Tricastin and Côtes du Vivarais are all well worth
considering if you're Winewise.

Then there's Châteauneuf-du-Pape (literally, the Pope's
new château). This sometimes great wine has been much
maligned in the past in Britain – 'another bottle of Château-

neuf, John' – when many of the Châteauneuf-du-Papes were
anonymous, blended, unauthentic rubbish. But now most
Châteauneuf-du-Papes available in Britain come from
single domaines or vineyards. Those bottled in the area of
production, generally a better bet, have an embossed motif
of crossed keys on the shoulder of the bottle and include
names like Domaine de Beaucastel, Château Rayas,
Domaine des Arnevels, Chanté Cigal, Mont Redon and
Vieux Télégraph. Most Châteauneuf is red, but there is
some white made – it can send you to your seventh heaven!

Also in the southern Rhône is a village called Beaumes
de Venise. It produces a full, meaty red wine but is most
famous for the dessert wine called Muscat de Beaumes de
Venise. This is a sweet powerful grapey white (normally
golden but sometimes slightly pinky) which goes really well
with fresh strawberries and raspberries. It's fortified, so
take care when drinking it – too much after lunch on a hot
day means that a three-hour siesta is essential!

Do you drink rosé wines? No, do I hear you say? Well, it's
about time you tried some Lirac or Tavel. The latter village
only makes rosé wines, although Lirac also makes red and
white. Both the rosés are deliciously fruity and dry, great
for slurping on a hot summer's day, sitting on the executive
punt. They are high in alcohol so, as with Muscat de
Beaumes de Venise, it's advisable to make sure a bed is
handy if you're going to drink more than a couple of glasses!

The Rhône is a very Winewise place – it provides a large
variety of different wines, from inexpensive village wines in
the south, the great wines of the north, sweet wines to dry
rosé, through to sparkling wine.

Provence – Sun-Drenched Beauties

I love the food and simply can't get enough of the garlic and
wonderful herbes de Provence. The area is full of delicious
restaurants at all levels, and the food from the markets is
something else. It's one of the few places in France where
you can buy fresh spices, lashings of garlic and all sorts of
chilli concoctions, not to mention the spiced local olives.

Any food served in Britain with any kind of Provençal
pretensions should be served with the regional wines. There
are several excellent Rosés de Provence, cool, crisp and dry
with just a touch of sweetness from the very ripe grapes.
Often you'll recognise them in shops by their skittle-shaped
bottles. Today, wine-making techniques have vastly
improved, and you don't get so many of the nasty hot burnt
wines that taste boiled and lack acidity. Just tasting a good
Provence rosé brings to mind the wonderful natural herb
and pine smells that seem to abound in the region.

Lots of really strong Provençal food calls out for powerful
red wines. Those made in Coteaux d'Aix-en-Provence are
big robust tannic wines, often with lots of good southern
flavoured fruit as well as a cedary wood flavour. There's one
château in particular, Château Vignelaure, whose proprie-
tor previously owned Château La Lagune in the Médoc in
Bordeaux. As a result he planted the blackcurrant-tasting
Cabernet Sauvignon variety and blends it with Syrah and
Grenache to make an exceptionally good red wine. It's more
expensive than most, but well worth the difference. If you're
into organic wines, this is one to go for, as it tells you on the
label that it's made without the use of insecticides and
chemical fertilisers. It's a very ethnic wine, like the best
from the VDQS area. In general the whites are fairly
disappointing, still hot and boiled, although there are a few
that are fine if drunk very young.

Look out for good red wines from the Appellations Bandol,
Cassis (not a bad way of describing the wine), Palette (a
tiny area) and Côtes de Provence, all of which produce good
beefy reds high in alcohol and fruit, and good easy drinking
rosés.

But if you're down there on holiday, simply try any of the Vin de Pays or VDQS red wines, as they're all fairly earthy and robust. Coteaux des Baux-en-Provence are worth paying a little extra for (although they're very cheap) and can be found around the colourful region of St Rémy de Provence. In particular, look out for the magnificent Domaine de Trevallon (available from Yapp Brothers – see Chapter 12, 'Bottle Stop'), a rich powerful red.

Côtes du Luberon is very much an up-and-coming Wine-wise area. One of the biggest and most impressive estates there, whose wines are widely distributed in Britain, is Château Val Joanis. They make excellent fruity whites and rosés, as well as slightly softer jammy reds (not unlike southern Côtes-du-Rhône wines), less robust than many of the more beefy red Provence wines. It's thought that this area will gain Appellation Contrôlée status soon and the price is bound to go up, so if you're Winewise you'll start buying these wines now.

On restaurant wine lists, Provençal wines are often a good bet as there are several relatively unknown properties whose wines are great value for money.

Among the most amazing sights in the south of France
are the sands and salt pans that lie to the east of Montpel-
lier. And it's not the beaches that make the area so unusual,
but the thousand hectares (1 hectare = 2.47 acres) of vines
actually planted in the sand. The owners, the innovative
Domaines Viticole des Salins du Midi (whose brand name is
Listel), not only own the largest area of vineyards in France
but are also the second largest salt producer in the world.

In between the rows of vines, barley is planted to help
prevent wind erosion of the very fine sand. Listel believe in
growing their vines as organically as possible, so they
plough the barley back into the sand as a natural fertiliser
as well as using manure from the Camargue horses they
keep on the estate. The wines are labelled Vin de Pays des
Sables du Golfe du Lion, as the area has not yet been
granted its own Appellation Contrôlée, though the quality
of Listel's wine certainly merits it.

Their winery has all the latest technology and rivals the
huge Californian installations. At Domaine de Jarras near
Aigues Mortes (which is open to visitors), they make their
unique Gris de Gris. This is a very delicately coloured pink
wine, lighter than a standard Provence rosé. It's made from
the first-run juice from the local Grenache and Cinsault
grapes. Crisp and dry but full of fruit it's very easy to drink.
Their whites are just as impressive – youthful and fresh,
without the smell of a wine made in a hot climate. Reds are
made with local grapes and increasingly with the classic
claret grape Cabernet Sauvignon. You will not be disappointed by any wine with the name Listel on the label.

My idea of Winewise bliss is eating sea food cooked in
garlic in the local restaurants, with a glass of Listel Gris de
Gris, and watching the thousands of flamingos flying by.
And in case you think you're seeing things, the water in the
salt pans really is pink ... when the salt is very concentrated, millions of tiny shrimps invade the water, giving it
a pink glow.

Alsace – The Spicy Treat

Alsace (or Alsacien) wines are very Winewise. The full name of the area is Alsace-Lorraine. Many people are not aware of the amazing value for money Alsacien wines offer. This is partly because the region has suffered from a form of schizophrenia, changing nationalities several times in its life. So you'd be forgiven if you're still not sure whether it's in France or Germany. Since the First World War, it's been part of France (apart from a few years during the Second World War), but to this day it retains a lot of German traits. If only they would change the bottle shape there might not be so much confusion.

Many people don't know what to expect when they buy a bottle of Alsace wine. Some mistakenly believe that they are all medium-sweet, similar to some German wines. But they are fermented dry and any apparent sweetness comes from the natural residual sugar within the grapes.

Alsace is a fairly narrow strip of land in between the Vosges mountains to the west, sloping east for eighteen miles to the Rhine and the German frontier. The whole area is about eighty miles long, ending in the south at the Swiss border. Although it's quite far north, Alsace doesn't have a high rainfall and benefits from warm, sunny summers. These help the grapes ripen and mean the area can consistently produce excellent dry whites. The south of Alsace, known as the Haut-Rhin, produces the best wines from vineyards planted on south and south-easterly slopes with maximum sun exposure.

Alsace wine labels are very logical, and the wines are labelled clearly. They carry the name of the grape variety on the label and contain 100 per cent of the specified variety, unlike other regions of France where they are generally allowed up to 15 per cent of another variety without stating it on the label.

The three widest-planted grape varieties, accounting for around 65 per cent of total production, are Gewürztraminer, Riesling and Sylvaner.

Gewürztraminer is the epitome of spiciness, and nobody

knows how to make it quite like the Alsaciens – it's what
Alsace is all about. The wines are very pungent and the
natural alcohol level is high. Rich in texture, high in
natural sugar although fermented dry, Gewürztraminer is
ideal with spicy, oriental food like the fiery Thai food and
many Chinese dishes. It's because it has such a concentrated
taste that it can cope with the mouth-burning chillies. In
very hot years, such as 1976, 1983 and 1985, Vendange
Tardive and Selection de Grains Nobles wines are made.
The grapes are harvested very late, often with the same
noble rot found in Sauternes. They shrivel up and the sugar
content (and therefore potential alcohol) rises to produce
fabulously luscious wines which are particularly attractive
when made from the Gewürztraminer.

Alsace Riesling can have more depth to it than its
German counterpart, and a more concentrated ripeness due
to warmer summers. It seems to be able to last for years
and years, and shows the versatility of the grape which can
also be delicious when drunk young. It accounts for over 20
per cent of Alsace vineyards, and plantings are increasing
all the time.

Sylvaner accounts for about 20 per cent of planting and
produces a light, dry aromatic wine, largely drunk locally.
It's pleasant but doesn't have the complexity of other
varieties.

Muscat is a very flowery grape without the heavy spiciness of the Gewürztraminer and generally produces more
'grapey' wines. But sometimes with young wines it can be
difficult to tell the two varieties apart. The wines, while
rich, tend to be less luscious than Gewürztraminer.

Pinot Gris, or Tokay, produces lightly spiced wines with
a flavour of ripe soft fruit. Depending on vintage and
producer it seems to be able to produce a wide variety of
styles.

Pinot Blanc is the lightest and least spicy of the Alsace
grapes. It produces green, refreshing dry wine best enjoyed
young with good acidity but without the concentration or
individuality of the other Alsace grapes.

Pinot Noir (the Burgundy grape) is the only red grape to

be grown in Alsace in any quantity, although it accounts
for only 5 per cent of the area's production. It produces
wines much lighter in colour than red Burgundy, with an
orangey-pinky hue. Old vintages, although rarely seen,
seem to take on more depth and richness and appear to have
matured very well – a characteristic they keep concealed
whilst young.

Look out for Alsace Grand Cru wines which come from
the best vineyards where yields are restricted and the wines
have to be passed by a tasting panel.

Alsace probably remains one of the most overlooked
quality-wine producing regions in France. And if you're
Winewise, you'll take the trouble to investigate these
French wines masquerading in German bottles, and will be
delighted by the results. In the past it has been difficult to
find any old or particularly unusual Alsace wines, but now
a new company, l'Alsacien in London's Old Brompton Road,
have added substantially to the spice of life (see Chapter 12,
'Bottle Stop').

Good winemakers to look out for include Beyer, Gisselbrecht, Hugel, Marc Kreydenweiss, Sick Dreyer and
Trimbach.

Chapter 18

Portugal –
Powerful and Punchy

This is the the most exciting Winewise part of the book. Portugal is now absolutely brilliant value for money, and be warned, it simply cannot stay like that for ever!

Forget the ubiquitous dumpy bottle full of medium-sweet rosé, and find out about the quality wines Portugal has on offer which are cheaper and more interesting. Since Portugal joined the EEC, we have seen lots of new wines coming over to Britain, all of which were previously unheard of and used to be consumed locally. Now led by the giant chain Sainsbury's, all leading supermarkets and wine merchants have their fingers on the Portuguese pulse. In general it's the red wines which are so good.

Look out for the words 'Garrafeira' on the label. This means the wine has been aged in bottle and will generally be much smoother. 'Reserva' is not as exact a term as it is in Spanish and generally means the company's best wine, although it's more of a marketing gimmick than an assurance of quality.

Look out for Douro reds, made in the port-making region from the same grapes. It's estimated that only 40 per cent of the Douro's production is fortified, the remainder being sold as Douro table wine. The wines are big, gutsy, full and dry, with the power of the flavour of port, without the sweetness and the added alcohol. These are wines ideal with spicy or gamey food as they can stand up to the flavour; they can be rather dry on their own.

Some of the best wines come from single properties (known as *quintas*) such as Quinta do Cotto. This family-run estate shows just how good Portuguese wines can be when made by a good winemaker. Owner Miguel Champalimaud believes that the 'burnt' taste that has characterised

Douro reds in the past is due to the uncleaned juice and yeasts left in the wine as well as the hot climate. The best Douro wines have intense fruit, exactly like the fruit found in a good Vintage Port but without the extra alcohol. Champalimaud also believes in ageing some of his wines in a proportion of new oak barrels, a practice rarely witnessed in Portugal. Look out for his wines: they include Lello Reserva, Quinta do Cotto and Grande Escolha (appropriately translated as 'best choice'). The last one is particularly Winewise – only 19,000 bottles on average are made each year and by the time it's ready to drink, the wine will be a classic and will no longer be on sale.

Because the region is so hot, many of the whites tend to be less successful, low in acidity, burnt on the nose and a little flabby.

Don't be put off if you find an older red vintage on a wine list, as these wines keep well and can improve with bottle age. Pound for pound per bottle, many Portuguese wines are better value than their French counterparts.

Look out for Dão wines (pronounced Dow-ng); again, the reds are the best. Full-bodied and tannic, these are not for the faint-hearted. They are big, robust, powerful wines (albeit less intense than Douro) delicious with food, although in a bid to make slightly softer, more accessible wines, the best co-operatives like Vinícola do Dão remove the tannic stalks before the grapes are pressed. In addition they buy in and blend grapes from a cooler area in the lowlands whose grapes have more fruit. Special wines like Reserva and Garrafeira are aged in wood. Most supermarkets now stock good examples.

One of the reasons that Portugal has been so slow to jump on the international wine bandwagon is that they have not in the past had the same efficiently run system as the French Appellation Contrôlée laws. Now they are gradually demarcating their regions and one of the most recent is Bairrada, to the west of Dão. Bairrada (By-rarder, as in larder) reds tend to be less tannic than Douro and Dão, with ripe tangy fruit. Older vintages take on a smoky flavour not unlike that found in old clarets.

Apart from areas which have been demarcated there are still several that only carry table wine status. In these regions the best Winewise idea is to look for the producer's name. Just south of Lisbon in a region known as Setúbal (pronounced Stuw-bal) two companies, J. M. da Fonseca and João Pires, are making superb wines. The latter has an Australian winemaker who is making excellent wines from Portugal's indigenous grapes and is also using some of the other European varieties, such as Cabernet Sauvignon and Chardonnay. These two companies produce some of Portugal's best whites as well, clean crisp wines with good acidity and flavour. Look out for them – they are sensational value for money, especially the João Pires Dry Muscat.

In the Ribatejo region, the huge co-operative at Almeirim is now making really Winewise wines. They make light, fruity reds, similar in weight to a Beaujolais. In the same region a family-owned estate is producing some exciting wines sold under the Dom Hermano label.

So the message is clear – get Winewise to Portugal. The wines are amazingly cheap at the moment but because of market forces cannot stay that way for ever, so experiment with them. Buy as much as you can of the reds and keep them for a few years – you'll thank me in years to come!

Chapter 19

Spain –
Flamenco Good Value

Spain is one of the most Wine-wise regions from which to buy. It's losing its plonk image and now offers a wide range of good value wines.

It was Rioja, the Spanish buzz word of the late 1970s, that helped put Spain back on the quality map. Rioja is one of the few Spanish regions to have been advertised generically in this country, hence its fame. Rioja quickly became known for its smooth, oaky-tasting reds which were excellent value compared to their French counterparts. It is one of the most organised wine regions of Spain, situated in the north of the country. It is no accident that traditional Rioja wines have similarities with Bordeaux. At the end of the last century when the hungry vine-eating louse, Phylloxera, destroyed the majority of the Bordeaux vineyards, many of that region's winemakers crossed the Pyrenees to Rioja.

They brought with them the idea of ageing wine in small (225-litre) oak casks, which is what gives Rioja its distinctive oaky taste. They were fortunate that the local grapes, the Tempranillo and Garnacha (related to the Grenache of the Rhône) made big, beefy wines whose flavour was enhanced by wood ageing.

The Spanish equivalent to a château is a bodega, a name you'll see on most Rioja labels. Just as anywhere else, each bodega has its own house style in winemaking and, when you find one you like, it's the name of the bodega you should try to remember rather than the vintage.

Now, sometimes for cashflow reasons, a new-style wine is coming in. Some producers are making wines that are not wood-aged and are therefore ready for drinking (and of course selling) much earlier. They are lighter, fruitier wines without the characteristic oaky/vanilla flavour.

It is worth noting that there are different classifications of Rioja, as they give a good indication of the style of wine to expect. They all relate to how the wine has been stored, or aged, which contributes a great deal to its taste.

All these terms, if not found on the main label, will appear on a back label authorised by the Spanish wine governing body. 'Sin Crianza' means without ageing, which indicates a light, forward style of wine. 'Crianza' means a short ageing period of one year in bottle – generally little or no time in wood, so it won't have the vanilla flavour.

'Reserva' (you'll generally find this on the main label) indicates that the wine has been aged for at least three years, of which at least one has been in wood. 'Gran Reserva' is the top classification, indicating a total of five years' ageing in oak barrels and bottle. These are generally the most full-bodied wines – and generally keep the longest. If you hold on to Reserva wines, they can become Gran Reserva in your own home once they have spent time in the bottle!

White Rioja is quite a different story. There are two distinctly different styles: the heavy, gold, nutty wines aged in wood and the crisp, dry, new-style wines. Unfortunately it is virtually impossible to tell from the label which style the wine is – it's back to knowing the particular style of wine a specific bodega is making. The only clue is that if the word 'Reserva' appears it will be one of the rich, nutty, wood-aged wines.

The new-wave whites are the ones I prefer, although one could argue, quite rightly, that they are not typical Rioja. But if they are pleasant to drink, who cares? They are made from one of Spain's most widely planted grapes, the Viura. Some of the best Riojas are made from the following bodegas: Rioja Alta, Marqués de Cáceres, Muga, CVNE, Marqués de Riscal, Olarra and Bodegas Riojanas. Rioja, while not the same amazing value it was in the 1970s, is still a Winewise buy.

Close to Rioja, but far less well known, is Navarra which, due to Rioja's hefty profile, has been put unfairly into the shade. Its wines are very similar, and made by the same

method from the same grape varieties. What is different is
the price! They are still a good bit cheaper than Rioja,
simply because they are less popular. Winewise readers
should investigate Navarra, noting the name of the bodega
when you find one you like. Again, the five- to ten-year-old
Reservas are the best Winewise buys, and the same classification applies as for Rioja. There are more reds than
whites available in Britain, but those whites that do make
it tend to be of the new-wave variety – clean, crisp and dry.

Spain's biggest white wine-producing area is in central
Spain, a vast area known as La Mancha. In the past, the
majority of wine produced here used to be distilled to make
industrial alcohol, which is little encouragement to producers and consumers alike! Now the best co-operatives have
invested in modern technology and can make temperature-
controlled dry, crisp whites rather than the traditional flat,
tired, oxidised wines of the past. The central area of La
Mancha, where the best whites come from, is Valdepeñas
(pronounced val de pain yas), not a familiar-sounding name,
but worth looking out for. They are also producing inexpensive fruity reds, which are extremely good value and excellent Winewise party wines.

But the most exciting wine area in Spain today is
Penedés, in the north-east. Here two leading producers,
Miguel Torres and Jean León, are making some fabulous
wines. They've been experimenting with French grape varieties and blending them with Spanish indigenous ones. The
results are stunning – big, beefy but well-balanced reds,
especially Torres Black Label made from Cabernet Sauvignon and Cabernet Franc.

Torres are using several white varieties, including the
spicy Gewürztraminer and Muscat (sold as Esmeralda) and
the classic Burgundy grape, Chardonnay. Aged in oak, the
results of the latter (sold under Torres Gran Viña Sol label)
are stunning.

What is so brilliant about the Penedés wines is that they
are excellent value for money. Look out for them in your
shops and try the different styles (the majority have very
helpful back labels describing the varieties used and how

the wine has been made). They are some of the best made wines in Spain, and I've yet to have a wine from either producer which was disappointing – more than can be said of many a more prestigious French wine region. Penedés is a really Winewise area to buy from.

In the same region, Cataluña, Spain's most successful sparkling wine, Cava, is made. In this region it is big business, and if you drive through the dramatic sandstone scenery, you will see several signs inviting you to visit the cellars of the biggest producers, namely Codorniu and Freixenet. Using a blend of grapes as the base, Cava is made by the time-consuming *méthode champenoise* which was explained earlier in the Champagne section. It has both a different aroma and flavour from that of Champagne because it's made from totally different grapes, but well-made Cava is delicious in its own right, and at roughly half the price of Champagne, cannot be ignored.

So if you're Winewise, you won't turn your nose up at Spain. In restaurants Spanish wines are often a far more Winewise buy than French.

Chapter 20

England –
Not At All British

There is one case where I would advise Winewise readers never to buy British. And before you stop reading, I don't mean that you shouldn't buy English wine. But despite the continual work of the Advertising Standards Board, it's a bit of a joke that the confusion between English and British wine should be allowed to exist. British wine is, in my view, a real consumer con. It is wine made from cheap imported concentrated grape must, often from Cyprus, which is brought into Britain and diluted to make 'wine'. So in reality there is nothing British about it at all.

All of which is a major affront to the entrepreneurial pioneers of *English* wine which has to be made from grapes grown in England. Not only do producers have to cope with the vagaries of the Great British climate, but they also have to contend with the great 'British Wine' scandal.

Obviously it's cheaper to grow grapes in hot climates such as Cyprus, but a further insult to English wine producers is that the government sees fit to charge higher duty rates on English wine than they do on the very much inferior, cheaper to produce, British wine. It's obvious that there are no MPs actually making English wine, otherwise this situation wouldn't exist. Bearing in mind the EEC protection of various generic terms such as Champagne, one would have thought that a government that incites one to 'buy British' would make sure that British *meant* British. They're obviously not Winewise!

Vines have been growing in Britain ever since Roman times, so it's not as if English wine is a new phenomenon. Many vineyards fell into disuse after the dissolution of the monasteries (the monks were quite partial to a bit of home-brewed table wine).

It was not until after the Second World War that interest in English vineyards was revived. Today there are over 1000 acres under vine and over 300 different producers. The latter are a hardy bunch, having to contend with climatic conditions which make their lives very difficult. In fact, Britain is one of the most northerly regions in the world growing vines. To get the best of available sunshine, the vast majority of English vineyards are situated in the south of England, especially in Kent and Sussex, although the most northerly vineyard which seems to survive is in Lincolnshire.

In addition, they don't have the traditional knowledge of winemaking that has been handed down from father to son in many other European vineyard areas. Originally, classic French grape varieties were planted, but it was soon realised that these were not best suited to the climate or the soil. Today most vineyards are planted with German varieties such as the high-cropping Müller-Thurgau, as well as some spicy varieties such as Schoenberger and Reichensteiner.

Most English wine is white, and I wouldn't advise Winewise readers to bother trying the red. The style of wine produced is naturally quite light, low in alcohol (because of the lack of sunshine), fairly acidic and either dry or medium dry. Producers are not best pleased when their wines are said to be Germanic in style. Many prefer to think of them as closer to the style of white wines made in the Loire valley although they're using German grape varieties, and this is certainly true of the top producers.

English wine might seem expensive, but if you take into account the fact that the duty and VAT account for well over a pound a bottle and that production costs are very high, it's not really so expensive. And the standard of winemaking has improved dramatically over the last few years. Some English wines are now even exported to the chauvinistic French!

So if you're feeling patriotic or want a good glass of dry white, give English wines a go. They tend to be best drunk young and you should be able to get an indication of their

style from the grape varieties often mentioned on the label.
The less dry ones can often be the most successful, as the
added sugar balances the naturally high acidity of a wine
made in a northern climate.

Look out for the EVA (English Vineyards Association)
seal of approval on the label, which indicates that the wine
has undergone and passed both tasting and analytical tests.
This is the closest English wine producers can get to a
recognition of quality, for the only permitted EEC classification is table wine. This is pretty unfair on the best
producers, who are making wines far above the quality of
European table wines.

Every year there is a competition called the Gore-Brown
Trophy, which awards gold and silver medals to the best
English wines. Winewise readers should look out for these
wines. Good vineyards include Carr-Taylor and Breaky
Bottom in Sussex; Lamberhurst, the biggest English vine-
yard, Biddenden and Spots Farm in Kent; Wootton in
Somerset; Three Choirs in Gloucestershire; Cavendish
Manor in Suffolk; Westbury in Berkshire; New Hall in
Essex; and Adgestone and Barton Manor on the Isle of
Wight. Most vineyards sell their wine from the vineyard
gate, and many are open to visitors during the summer, so
you can taste before you buy.

Some of the supermarkets are now selling English wine
at very competitive prices, so if you want to be Winewise,
make sure you cash in there too. I would much prefer to
drink a good English wine than a bland, commercial
German wine like Liebfraumilch. If you're Winewise, I
think you'd agree with me.

Chapter 21

Italy –
Pasta Partners

Until recently Italy was definitely not Winewise, even
though it is the biggest wine producer in the world, producing
around 8 billion litres a year. In the
past, it has always gone for quantity, rather than quality,
and the regulations that were in force (DOC – Denominazione di Origine Controllata, similar to the French Appellation Contrôlée) were largely ignored. The most dramatic
example of this was the 1986 methanol scandal where
illegal and poisonous methanol was added which actually
killed consumers.

But it is possible to be Winewise with Italian wines,
because a few dedicated producers are making good quality
wines. Indeed, some of them have decided not to operate
within the DOC system because, in their opinion, it restricts
them to local grapes which do not always produce the best
quality wines.

In fact, the majority of Italian wines are classified as
simple 'table wines', only 10–12 per cent of the total being
DOC or DOCG (Denominazione di Origine Controllata Garantita) wines, of which there are 220 different zones and
over 500 different wines.

The famous five – Frascati, Soave, Valpolicella, Chianti
and Lambrusco – have probably sent producers counting
their millions of lire all the way to the bank, but they
haven't really done a lot for the quality reputation of Italian
wines. There are plenty of other wines from elsewhere in
Italy that are better value.

The best way to become Winewise about Italian wines is
to buy them either from one of the leading supermarkets
(Sainsbury's, Waitrose or Tesco), all of whom offer excellent
own-label Italian wines, or from a specialist wine merchant.

The best of the latter is the chain of shops called The Market, in London, and, in particular, one known as Wine-cellars in Clapham. These are run by Nick Belfrage, Master of Wine. His staff are able to give expert advice on every aspect of becoming Winewise, Italian style.

So what follows is simply a brief guide to the wines from the most commonly seen regions from north to south.

Trentino

Confusingly, this region is also known as Alto Adige and Sudtirol. This is the most northerly part of Italy where German is often the first language, and many of the wines are quite Germanic in that they're very perfumed and they use some of the same varieties. As a result it makes it even more complicated when they label them in German. There are lots of grape varieties here such as Riesling, Pinot Blanc and Muscat, to name but a few of the white varieties.

But in my view the most interesting Winewise wines coming out of this region are the ones made from that star grape, Chardonnay. They tend to be much lighter than their New World or French counterparts but still have the citrus, whitecurrant zing of Chardonnay. Some of the Gewürztraminer wines (known as Traminer) are good buys if you like the spice of the grape but don't like the weighty wines it can produce elsewhere.

Most of the Trentino's production (80 per cent) is of red wine which is fairly light and fruity. As yet they are not very Winewise, although more interesting classic French grape varieties are being planted, and it's an area worth watching.

Veneto

Veneto is one of the prettiest regions of Italy, producing two of the best-known high-production wines: Soave and Valpolicella. Soave is made from the Trebbiano (Ugni Blanc) grape, not noted for producing wines with much character, either in France or in Italy. The best examples are from small, single estates which are just beginning to find their

way into Britain. A Winewise alternative is Bianco di
Custoza, a crisp, zippy white.

Valpolicella and Bardolino, made from a large number of
local grapes, are generally unexciting, both light and fruity,
although Valpolicella is slightly heavier. Again, the best
ones come from smaller producers and although there's no
guarantee, the word 'Classico' on the label sometimes indicates better quality.

One of the more bizarre products of Veneto is Reciotto
della Valpolicella Amarone – a fully flavoured wine made
from dried-up grapes. It's a sweet and sour taste that you
either love or hate.

Piedmont

Piedmont produces big, heavy, tarry reds such as Barolo
and Barbaresco, wines that often seem to have more tough
tannin than they do fruit. But older, more mature bottles
can be very Winewise, as they are not that expensive.
Barolo is generally regarded as one of Italy's top wines. But
don't get these confused with Barbera from the same region,
which is a light, rather acidic, glugging red.

This region also produces Dolcetto, a bizarre sweet, cho-
colatey red which is very definitely an acquired taste (which
many people never manage to acquire!). Italy's most famous
(or infamous) sparkling wine, Asti Spumante, is also made
here. But a more Winewise alternative is the sparkling
Moscato d'Asti, which is light, fizzy and spicy.

Friuli

Friuli has the potential to become one of Italy's most
Winewise regions. Whilst there is a confusing array of
styles and grape varieties, the most exciting wines are those
made from French varieties like Cabernet Franc, Merlot,
Malbec, Chardonnay, Sauvignon and Pinot Blanc (Bianco).
The independent producers really score here, making some
delicious wines.

Sainsbury's stock a red Cabernet Franc, quite soft and

light but flavourful, and Tocai Friulano, a fresh, dry white.
Both are from the Aquileia area of Friuli.

Emilia-Romagnia

Emilia-Romagnia, in central Italy at the top of the boot, is
the home of Lambrusco. This fizzy tipple comes in every
style from dry to sweet, in red or white, and should be low
in alcohol. It sells in huge amounts, possibly because it is so
cheap. The dry white version can be good value if served
well chilled. But other, more interesting, wines from this
region include those made from French varieties like soft
red Merlots and crisp dry Sauvignons, as well as a whole
host of Italian grape varieties.

Tuscany

Tuscany produces mainly red wines, the most famous (or
notorious) of which is Chianti, whose quality varies greatly.
If possible, you have to try to remember the producer's name
of one that you like, and single-vineyard versions tend to be
the best. Chianti is probably best drunk young rather than
keeping it for years and years.

But more interesting from this region is the exciting, full-
bodied and full-of-fruit (rather than just full of tannin)
Brunello di Montepulciano and, better still, the violet-
flavoured, powerful red Vino Nobile di Montepulciano.

Another wine that must be mentioned, one of Italy's most
exciting, is Antinori's Tignanello. This is a great example
of a producer making wine outside the DOC framework – it
has a high proportion of Cabernet Sauvignon (10–15 per
cent) and therefore cannot be classified and is known only
as 'table wine'. Tignanello is very Winewise, but the producers know it and it's no longer as cheap as it was.

Another wine worth checking out is Carmignano, which
is similar to Chianti but with a proportion of Cabernet
Sauvignon.

There are few good white wines produced in the region,
although some innovative producers are now making cold
fermented dry white wines.

Latium

Winewise travellers to Italy are advised to go to Latium, the area surrounding Rome, for its scenery rather than its wines. Its best-known wine is Frascati, a dry or off-dry white wine that can be insipid unless from a top producer. Better value can be found elsewhere.

Part of Umbria, to the north, extends into this region and Orvieto wines are worth a try as they're clean, floral whites which are mainly dry, but if the word 'abboccato' appears on the label, will be sweet.

Southern Italy and Sicily

Southern Italy is best avoided and there are few Winewise Sicilian wines. But one is Regaleali, a soft, perfumed, red table wine. The white is crisp, floral and dry, with a percentage of zingy Sauvignon. Then there's Marsala, a heavy, raisiny, sweet (or dry) wine which is often fortified.

The Winewise message about Italy is that if you are very selective you can find excellent wines that are often best drunk with Italy's delicious food.

Chapter 22

Germany –
Life
Beyond
Liebfraumilch

German wines are well known in Britain. The ubiquitous Liebfraumilch can be seen in almost every off-licence and supermarket. It's innocuous, fairly bland wine which sells in huge quantities. It's not particularly Winewise – Liebfraumilch is sold purely on price (not on quality) and the brands are heavily (and cleverly) marketed at premium prices. There's no reason why people shouldn't drink these wines – they're light, medium dry, fruity wines which can hardly give offence. But the reader is looking for something with more character and style, often for the same price.

There are Winewise bargains to be had from Germany – in fact Germany produces scores of really high quality wines at bargain prices. For years we the British have been spending millions of pounds on Liebfraumilch – a wine virtually unheard of (and certainly not drunk) in Germany. Now it's time we did ourselves the favour of buying some of the better quality wines – we deserve it!

But one of Germany's problems is that 99 per cent of the wine is white – there's no red to give any variation – and many of the wines have very similar styles, varying from dry to very sweet.

Germany has a northerly climate, the result being that its wines are generally lower in alcohol than French ones (because of the lower natural sugar content of the grape). In many wines the high acidity level, the result of unripe grapes, is clumsily disguised by the addition of sugar to produce an unbalanced medium dry (or medium sweet) wine.

German wines find themselves in a strange state of limbo. Once drinkers have progressed from Liebfraumilch, they tend to go for drier wines, which leads them back to France.

It's only if they get really interested in wine that they
return to the interesting, top-of-the-range single-estate
German wines.

But perhaps one of the problems is to decide when to
drink German wines. They are fine chilled on a hot summer's day or served as an aperitif, but all the way through
a meal? This is where they lose marks for versatility and
the French, Spanish and Italians win hands down.

Germany's main advantage is that it produces white
wines which can be sparkling (a good Sekt is a Winewise
alternative to Champagne), dry (refreshing Trockens),
medium sweet (Kabinett) or ultra-sweet (Trockenbeerenauslese). And every degree of sweetness in between. But it's
important to buy one from a quality-conscious, small
producer.

However, this is not easy. Apart from Liebfraumilch,
merchants find it hard to sell any of Germany's quality
wines. They lament that they simply can't understand it.
The problem is that we, the punters, can't understand the
labels either! Even if you happen to be an expert in deci-
phering curly Gothic script, the masses of unpronounceable
names make life extremely difficult for even the most
dedicated Winewise reader. In the time it takes to work out
what the label says, you could have almost drunk the bottle
although, even then, you'd probably be none the wiser as to
the exact name of the wine. Although their labels are very
logical, they contain too much information to make them
easily recognisable. That's probably why the brands with
English names sell in such vast quantities.

In general the most exciting wines tend not to be among
the cheaper wines. But, if you like sweet wines which are
not as heavy as French wines, there are some good value
Auslese, Spätlese, Beerenauslese and Trockenbeerenauslese wines that, because few people buy them, can often be
the bargain on the wine list. All these names correspond to
the amount of natural sugar recorded in the grape when
harvested. In Germany, the higher the count the higher the
classification. QbA is the basic quality, QmP, Kabinett, next
Auslese, then Spätlese and Trockenbeerenauslese (not to be

confused with the word Trocken, which indicates a dry
wine). But apart from the last one, which will always be
sweet, even these terms can be confusing, as you can find
Auslese and Spätlese wines which taste dry, as the high
sugar has been removed from the wine during fermentation.
Yet more confusion!

In fact, the way of classifying quality in German wines
was the reason for the diethylene glycol (DEG) scandal.
Anti-freeze, for this is the normal name for DEG, makes
any wine to which it is added sweeter and more viscous. So
some nefarious winemakers in Austria and Germany added
it to their wines, obtaining higher prices by fooling the
authorities.

The greatest German wines are all made from the Riesling grape, which has a tendency to develop rich, oily fruit,
but standard German blends are usually made from the
high-cropping Müller-Thurgau. Eiswein is a rare sweet
wine, made from frozen shrivelled grapes with a very high
sugar content which are harvested in December and January, often when there is snow on the ground.

Don't bother with red German wine: it's generally thin
and uninteresting, suffering from the lack of sunshine.

If you visit the wine-producing areas in Germany it's
difficult to imagine who ever had the crazy idea of planting
the grapes in the first place. They can't have been Winewise,
or so you'd think! The steep slopes make cultivation and
picking extremely difficult. It's not unknown for harvesters
to have to wear climbing robes when picking! But while the
German winemakers are well up on technical know-how,
they are far less scrupulous about yields from their vineyards. In general, the greatest wines in the world are made
when the yield is restricted, and this is an integral part of
the French Appellation Contrôlée laws. But some German
producers go for quantity and not quality (they have to keep
the Great British public supplied with plonk), and as a
result some wines are very dilute.

Pay particular attention to the price of the well-known
brand names. Just because people feel secure, they pay well
over the odds for them; how else could the manufacturers

possibly afford the massive advertising campaigns that ensure they become household names? Winewise readers will know better than to pay through the nose for bad value simply because the wine has a media profile. Indeed many wine bars, restaurant lists and wine shops have a high mark-up on Liebfraumilch, which in turn subsidises the better-quality wines, which are better value. Don't subsidise the better wines, buy them and enjoy them!

Specialist wine merchants are the best bet here, as they can describe the various styles of wines on offer. To get the most out of German wines, it really is worth trading up from Liebfraumilch. You may well be surprised that for only a little more money you'll get a much nicer wine.

German growers to look out for: Schloss Reinhartshausen, Deinhard, Von Buhl, Bürklin-Wolf, Schubert, Friedrich Wilhelm Gymnasium, Müller, J. J. Prüm, Bischöfliche Priesterseminar.

Chapter 23

Bulgaria –
A Chip Off the Old
Bloc

Bulgarian wine is a brilliant Winewise buy, although it might not be the obvious wine-producing country to spring to mind. But the Winewise drinker will know that it's difficult to find such good value elsewhere. It's only relatively recently that the Eastern Bloc have got their wine-producing act together, and Bulgaria is now the fifth biggest wine exporter in the world.

Although miles and cultures apart, Bulgaria has not been slow in taking advantage of the world's buzz grape varieties, Cabernet Sauvignon, Merlot, Chardonnay, Riesling and Muscat. They've done a brilliant marketing exercise, and bargain Bulgarian bottles can be found in supermarkets all over Britain. They're virtually the cheapest bottles on the shelf.

The red Cabernet Sauvignon is medium-bodied with lots of blackcurrant-tasting fruit and the Merlot slightly softer and rounder. The Chardonnay has good lightweight, buttery fruit and is definitely the cheapest example of authentic Chardonnay to be found in the whole wide world. Look out for the flowery Riesling, which has good acidity or the steely Sauvignon Blanc. Also look out for Mehana white and red, both made from a blend of grapes, or Sakar Mountain Cabernet and Khan Krum Reserve Chardonnay.

Anyone who is really Winewise will always have a few Bulgarian bottles in their basement or under their bed (or wherever their cellar happens to be!). Make the most of these Slovak Slurps.

Chapter 24

Australia –
Down Under Sport

No it's not all cans of Fosters, Castlemaine XXXX and a Crocodile Dundee life! These ex-convicts (well some of their ancestors were anyway) really know how to make good wines. They have one of the best wine-making schools in the world, and a climate which doesn't produce duff vintages. Currently they are brilliant value for money, due to the exchange rate and the fact that in such a sunny climate they are producing so much wine they've now got a wine lake. And it certainly surprised me to learn that it costs only 20 pence more to ship a case from Australia than from Bordeaux. I only wish the difference in the airfares was as small!

The biggest wine-producing areas are in southern Australia: the Hunter Valley in New South Wales north of Sydney; Victoria, north of Melbourne; and the Barossa Valley, Murray River Valley and Coonawarra in South Australia. But what is more important than working out where all the regions are is deciding which styles of wine you like.

The Aussies make it relatively easy for us by their really Winewise labels, as, unlike the French, who seem to assume everyone should know, they tell you exactly what grapes are in the wine, which gives you a good indication of the style. In many ways it's easier to latch onto grape varieties and various producers' names rather than feeling you have to put your geography to the test.

In the past a lot of the wine produced was very alcoholic and heavy (entirely suitable for the fast-guzzling Aussies!), and many wines were actually fortified to make them even stronger. The new wave of winemakers has put an end to this, and more elegant-style wines are now coming up from Down Under.

It's the Chardonnay grape that is the megastar here (see Chapter 6, 'Grape Expectations'), producing rich, buttery, dry whites, quite some of the best Chardonnay-based wines in the world. There are two different styles: those made in stainless steel, which are fresh and zippy with a weighty citrus tang, and the bigger ones, aged in oak casks which give the wine a toasted aroma and have more full-bodied fruit. Note the name of the producer whose wine you like.

Even the most expensive are cheaper than many white Burgundies made from the same grape. And, whilst some people would say they never have as much complexity, they are absolutely jam-packed full with powerful, punchy fruit. Most of the time many of us are looking for that obvious upfront flavour which makes the wine immediately enjoyable.

One of the best around is Rosemount from the Hunter Valley, especially their Show Reserve made from the best grapes. In lots of wine bars and restaurants Australian Chardonnay is a very Winewise choice, as there appear to be few badly made wines imported into Britain, something one can't say for French, German or Spanish wines.

Look out for Barossa Valley Rhine Rieslings sold in the infamous German-lookalike fluted bottle. These are lightly aromatic wines which are off-dry, but with a touch of sweetness from the natural residual sugar in the grape. They've got good floral character and are easy drinking wines. Pound for pound per bottle, they have a lot more character than similarly priced German counterparts.

The Semillon grape, used in making dry white Bordeaux, produces good wines in this climate. Again, it's quite full-bodied with rich, oily fruit. The wood-aged examples are the most interesting, as they take on a richer, more complex, almost creamy flavour. Australia is one of the few countries to look at Semillon seriously. Their results show how worthwhile this is.

The classic gooseberry-flavoured Sauvignon Blanc grape used in Sancerre is now producing some good Aussie wines. They have a flinty type of flavour and good acidity. In the future we should start to see more of them in our shops.

For lovers of sticky Australian wines, late-picked or liqueur Muscats are a must. This intensely aromatic grape seems to go even more over the top when grown under lots of sunshine. The best Muscats come from Victoria and are wonderfully rich, great for any type of pudding, but watch out as they have been fortified and are therefore very high in alcohol. They're an unusual alternative to Madeira or Port.

Some producers also make dry Muscat: elegant, mid-weight, flowery wines which give you the sensation of Muscat but without the texture or the sweetness.

Chardonnay's red-blooded brother is the blockbusting Shiraz grape, known as Syrah in the Rhône valley in France. The wines produced from it are not dissimilar in style to big Rhône wines except that, due to the hotter climate, they tend to have less hard tannin and softer, lighter, albeit powerful fruit.

Shiraz is often blended with the classic claret grape Cabernet Sauvignon, which contributes an intense black-currant aroma rather like Ribena. The commercial blends which are currently available under several supermarkets' own-labels are brilliant quaffing wines. Their ripe, smooth, plummy and blackcurrant flavour makes them worryingly easy to drink. If you're drinking a red wine without food, it's sometimes nice to down a glass or two of smooth red without giving your teeth a tannin bath. But some Cabernet/Shiraz blends, especially those that have been aged in wood, are much bigger wines, ideal to keep for a few years or to drink with food.

Grenache, another Rhône grape, is used to produce a lot of the cheap everyday wines, but little of it gets to Britain. And although some people have been experimenting with the Burgundian Pinot Noir grape, if you're a fan of this variety it's best to stick to Burgundy.

Although unfortunately not widely available in Britain, one of the most Winewise buys in Aussie wine is their bag-in-box wines. In fact, in order to cope with their gulping masses, they can lay claim to having pioneered this pack-aging technique. And although they sometimes refer to them as 'bladder' wines they did have the sense to bag decent wine in the first place. So if you're looking for a bag-in-box wine, don't forget to look Down Under.

Most of the supermarket own-label brands are very relia-ble. If you want to pay a little more for less commercial-style wines, names to look out for include Hardy, Geoff

Merril, Hill Smith, Wynns, Lindeman, Penfold's, Pira-
mimma, Yalumba, Orlando and Berri Estates in South
Australia, Rosemount, Rothbury, Tyrrell and de Bortoli in
New South Wales and Tyrrell, Taltarni and Brown Broth-
ers. In Western Australia, look out for wines from Houghton
Supreme.

Australia just cannot be ignored if you're Winewise.

Chapter 25

New Zealand –
The Wines are not
Extinct

Heard of Kiwi wine? You have now, and no, it's not extinct! If you're Winewise, you'll remember that there's a lot more to New Zealand than butter, lamb and kiwis. It tends to get forgotten as a wine-producing country, because up until quite recently very little of the wine was exported. Many people liken its wines to those of Australia. This is a complete mistake, as these two countries are in fact 1,300 miles apart, the same distance as between London and Moscow. New Zealand has a much cooler climate than Australia, and as a result the wines produced are totally different. The climate has probably got more in common with that of Germany – essentially cool.

This century the vineyards had almost disappeared because of the vine-eating bug Phylloxera and the over-zealous temperance movement. The wine industry only survived due to the influx of thirsty American servicemen stationed in New Zealand during the Second World War, although the foundations of the modern New Zealand wine industry had been laid early in the twentieth century by emigrants from Yugoslavia and the Lebanon.

The most widely planted grape variety is the German Müller-Thurgau, which produces both dry and medium-dry whites. But what is really exciting is that they've now planted lots of classic French varieties and are making some really interesting Winewise wines which are not expensive.

Look out for spicy Gewürztraminer, lighter than the Alsace variety, and the white Riesling, a grape that seems to perform well in the cool climate. But the star of the show is the charming Chardonnay, which is making lighter wines than those of Burgundy but which are pleasing both to the palate and the purse.

If you are fed up with paying inflated prices for Sancerre from the Loire, try a New Zealand Fumé Blanc or Sauvignon Blanc, which has almost more Sancerre-like characteristics than the real thing. Another Loire grape, the versatile Chenin Blanc, fares well in New Zealand, and the resulting wines don't tend to develop that musty smell of Chenin (see Chapter 6, 'Grape Expectations').

Red grapes used include the well-travelled Cabernet Sauvignon, the less prolific Pinot Noir and the rich tannic Pinotage.

Sunny Marlborough (and no, the wines do not have a smoky flavour!) in the north of South Island is now the third largest grape-growing area, even though it's a relative newcomer. Names to look out for include pioneer producers Montana and Penfold's, both of whose wines are widely available in Britain.

The same two companies also have wineries in the largest grape-growing region, Gisborne, north-east of North Island. Look out for Cook's wines, including their excellent generic whites and reds, as well as Chenin Blanc and Cabernet Sauvignon from Hawkes Bay, the second-largest vineyard area in New Zealand. Other top producers are Delegats, Nobilo, Matua, Selak and Morton.

As New Zealand is in the southern hemisphere the grapes are harvested in March and April, which means you can beat the Beaujolais Nouveau hype by buying the current vintage while European grapes are hardly in flower. Great Winewise one-upmanship!

It looks certain that sales of quality New Zealand wines are going to continue to grow as they are such good value. Make sure you are Winewise enough to cash in on them.

Chapter 26

California –
A Sunny State of Mind

Everything about California is upfront, from the film stars and the lifestyle to the wines. And because of the warm climate, California is able to produce vast quantities of wine from all sorts of grape varieties. In fact it had to be the Americans who coined the phrase 'varietal' to describe wines made from a single grape variety.

But Americans like to know just about as much as possible about what they're eating and drinking, a fetish which is quite helpful to the Winewise drinker. If you can take the time to read all the small print on a California wine label you'll probably discover which row of the vineyard the wine came from, not to mention a string of additives or treatments the wine has seen!

Stating the grape variety makes it easier to make a Winewise choice of California wines. The wine must be at least 75 per cent of the stated grape variety; if not, it will simply show the name of the brand or the producer. Labels also detail alcohol content, often up to 14 per cent, and many will give the sugar content, particularly if they are slightly sweeter whites like Johannisberg Riesling and Gewürztraminer. If the area is mentioned, it means at least 85 per cent of the grapes have come from the specified region.

In many cases the Californians have led the world in winemaking technology, especially as a result of research at their winemaking College at the University of California, Davis. They've discovered how to do most things bigger and better than the rest of Europe, certainly in technical terms, anyway. In the past, because of the heat, many California wines were high-alcohol blockbusters, heavy, often with over-ripe fruit and low acidity. But now producers have realised that the wine-drinking public is not looking for strong, overpowering wines. So, with the help of their home-grown, highly competent winemakers trained at the University of California, Davis, top producers are now making more elegant, European-style wines.

Most of California's wine production comes from the scorching hot Central Valley. These 'jug wines' are the kind sold in vast quantities in carafes and are of passable quality. Controlled by five major companies, oenologists have now discovered ways of producing much lighter, less alcoholic wines. One such company is Gallo, said to have the biggest winery in the world. But the main quality-wine producing areas are the Napa Valley, Sonoma, Mendocino and south of San Francisco. Here the smaller producers (by their terms) are known as 'boutique' wineries, and they make 'designer' wines.

The rave grape varieties are the white Chardonnay, of

Burgundy fame, and the red Cabernet Sauvignon from
Bordeaux. Many of the top Chardonnays are aged in wood
and take on a rich, buttery, toasted flavour. The best can be
kept for several years. They tend to mature much faster
than their European counterparts and have a very pungent
and concentrated flavour.

The top Sauvignon Blancs (or Fumé Blancs) are crisp,
dry, fragrant wines which can benefit from some time in
oak. But the young, fresh gooseberry-tasting styles easily
rival Sancerre. They also make more floral, peachy wines
from the Johannisberg Riesling which can be dry with good
acidity or, if late harvested, rich and luscious. And the
Chenin Blanc (a recent introduction) makes much lighter,
dry, appley-flavoured wines which seem to have more zing
and acidity than those grown in the Loire. They're best
drunk young. There's also some sparkling wine made in the
Napa, but whilst the best, Schramsberg, is delicious, it's not
very Winewise because of its price, far higher than that of
Champagne.

The reds made from Cabernet Sauvignon were originally
big and blackcurranty with a minty, eucalyptus aroma, but
now many producers are softening up the wines by adding
some Merlot to make the wines more attractive for earlier
drinking. The majority of boutique wines are aged in wood,
generally French oak. American oak gives the wine a much
more pungent, often 'over-oaked' flavour.

They've had nothing like as much success with the awkward Pinot Noir, which, however hard producers try, does
not seem to be able to produce wines of anything like the
quality of good red Burgundy.

But it's the Zinfandel, the most widely planted red, which
seems to be able to produce all styles of wine from a light,
thin, nouveau-style wine to a heavier, very concentrated
and high-alcohol, port-like wine. A Winewise indication of
the wine's style can be to check the alcohol level, always
given on California wine labels. Top-quality Zinfandel from
the best producers is a wine to keep rather than to drink
immediately as it will improve with age. And it can be a
Winewise bargain, because it's nothing like as well known

or as popular as the other Californian varieties. You can
also find 'white' Zinfandel, although to most people who
aren't colour-blind it looks like a light rosé. Confused? It's
what the Californians rather preciously call a 'blush' wine,
simply a marketing man's new term for light rosé, which
appeals to their health-conscious way of life because it's low
in alcohol.

Some of the top producers include Mondavi, Chalone,
Château St Jean, Clos du Val, Edna Valley, Heitz, Iron
Horse, Jordan, Paul Masson (they make varietal wines as
well as their carafes), Joseph Phelps, Ridge Vineyards,
Rutherford Hill, Schramsberg, Stag's Leap, Trefethen Vine-
yards and Mark West Vineyards.

As with Burgundy, remember the name of the producer
or vineyard, and experiment with wines made from other
grape varieties from the same property. Also, remember
that because of the constant climate, vintages in California
are less important than Europe.

Chapter 27

Chile –
Hot Stuff

There are now many Winewise buys to be had from Chile in South America. The wines are big and powerful, with masses of fruit. Miguel Torres of Spanish Penedés fame also have vineyards there, and are producing some stunning wines under the Santa Digna label.

The red Cabernet Sauvignons are big, rich, jammy reds with slightly sweet, blackcurrant-flavoured fruit – very Winewise. They are excellent with spicy food – especially chilli beans!

New-wave whites are made from Chardonnay, with medium-weight fruit, and Sauvignon Blanc, crisp, clean and zippy – both good varietals. Semillon is the most widely planted white, which can produce rich oily wines or clean crisp drier ones more akin to their Australian counterparts.

Look out for wines from Concha y Toro (their Cabernet Sauvignon bag-in-box is excellent), Cousiño Macul, Linderos and Torres.

So give Chile a try – the quality is extremely Winewise.

Chapter 28

A Fortified Tale

Fortified wine is wine strengthened by the addition of alcohol. I heard a story the other day about a new employee in a brewery who didn't quite understand this. She was given the job of putting together a wine list for a restaurant customer, grouping all the wines under their respective headings. When her boss read it, he wondered where all the clarets had gone. He soon found out when he turned to the 'fortified' section – they were *all* there! When the luckless girl was asked to explain this inexplicable error, it turned out that she thought that as castles were fortified buildings, all châteaux would be fortified wines!

Sherry

One of the best-known fortified wines is sherry, looked on by many as being the drink you offer the vicar and aunt or get thrust into your hand at your granny's 81st birthday. But there's a lot more to it than the schooners and tacky draught-barrelled variety seen in so many pubs. Due to inefficient and totally unfair EEC legislation, an awful lot of wine sold with the word 'sherry' on the label has nothing to do with the real McCoy. Unlike Champagne producers, the sherry producers of Jerez (which is where the name originated) did not get their act together to prevent other countries using their name. As a result you'll find in the shops Cyprus, South African, not to mention the dreaded 'British' sherry, which appeal to many people because of their attractive prices. The combination of the words 'British' and sherry are an insult to both parties. The closest British sherry comes to being 'British' is when imported grape must is diluted in this country. The situation is a consumer con and a disgrace – just like 'British' wine. And the Spanish, as you can imagine, are none too pleased either. But authentic sherry is a Winewise buy if you know what to look for.

A chilled glass of Fino, the driest of the styles, is a delicious Winewise drink. A really good example will be bone-dry with a nutty flavour and refreshing acidic zing to it. Try it with (or in) rich gamey soups – it's a good combination. Manzanilla is a type of Fino with a salty tang said to derive from the seawinds in Sanlucár de Barrameda, the region where it's made. This is definitely a Winewise sherry.

Amontillado is a mature Fino which has become darker in colour and has richer fruit, although many commercial Amontillados have been sugared up to please what's thought to be the great British taste.

Oloroso is darker and stronger than Fino, and is generally sweetened to make a richer sherry. Old Olorosos are well worth looking out for, as the sweetness fades, leaving a deliciously rich but dry, tasty sherry.

Then there's Cream Sherry, still the biggest-selling sherry, accounting for over a third of all sales in Britain. A good Cream Sherry will be sweet but will also be balanced by a kick of acidity to prevent a sickly-sweet cloying taste.

For a really individual style of sherry, try an Almacenista (pronounced Almatheneesta). This type of sherry comes from small stockholders who mature their own wines. As a result they are individual in style and generally delicious. The best come from Lustau and are made in all the above styles.

Producers to look out for include Lustau, Domecq, Valdespino and Barbadillo.

Port

Powerful punchy Port is generally portrayed as having great hangover potential, and for those who like powerful after-dinner drinks, Port takes some beating. But the hangover story is not strictly true; it's more that it's generally the last thing you can remember drinking, and therefore gets the blame for the gin and tonics, cans of Fosters, Champagne, red and white wine etc. you'd already knocked back before you'd even thought about the Port.

But it's true that Port is much stronger than wine because it's fortified with alcohol. This results not only in increased strength, but a natural sweetness from the grapes is noticeable. This would have been transformed into alcohol, and therefore made a drier wine, if the spirit had not been added to arrest fermentation.

Port is produced in the Douro valley in Portugal, probably the most impressive and magical wine region to visit. Very steep, terraced vineyards slope down hundreds of feet to the river Douro and all the Port companies have houses strategically placed with breathtaking views of the valley. The population is very sparse, and you're unlikely to spy another dwelling from the terrace of one of these houses. It's a very hot area, producing powerful grapes which are naturally high in sugar and therefore potential alcohol. In many ways it's not dissimilar to the Rhône Valley in France.

It has suffered a bit from its old wave image – crusty old colonels in their clubs passing the Port. But the Port producers have not been blind to this and have launched several new types of Port, more suitable for those of us who have to go back to work after lunch.

If you want to go really over the top, buy a Vintage Port (a bottle will set you back the price of a good restaurant meal). But although still popular in Britain, this only represents a tiny percentage of Port houses' production. It's wine made from one single year which the houses have 'declared' as being of good enough quality. Vintages currently available include 1963, 1966, 1967, 1970, 1975, 1980, 1982, 1983 and 1985.

Genuine Vintage Port is bottled after two years' maturation in wood and therefore throws a sediment in bottle while it is still maturing. This is why you need to decant Vintage Port unless you like to use your teeth as a filter to remove the bits! Before decanting, try to leave the bottle standing upright so that the sediment will settle at the bottom. Then tilt it slowly and gently, pouring the wine into the decanter over a light, and stop pouring when the sediment reaches the neck of the bottle. If you've got a shaky hand, or the bottle has recently been moved, there is a much easier alternative. Get a jug and a coffee filter and pour the Port relatively slowly into it. Whilst sometimes frowned on by the old school, this is a Winewise short cut!

But Vintage Port is expensive and, what's more, once it's been decanted, it really needs to be drunk within the day (hence the hangovers) and it's relatively heavy. But there are several Winewise alternatives. Try Vintage Character Port, which is what it says – the same style as a Vintage but about a quarter of the price. It has been matured for longer in wood and therefore doesn't throw a sediment. It's made from a blend of different vintages and is nothing like as heavy as Vintage Port, while it's still got a good flavour. It also has the advantage (or disadvantage, depending on which way you look at it!) of not having to be drunk at one go. An opened bottle with the cork pushed back in can last for about three months. It's definitely a Winewise buy!

Or try a Late Bottled Vintage Port. This is Port from one year (generally not the 'declared' Vintage years) which has been aged in wood and is bottled much later than Vintage Port. As a result it contains no sediment and is rather like a mini Vintage Port. While it doesn't have the depth and concentration it is a good, lighter, tasty version.

You can also find Tawny Ports which have an indication of the age of the youngest wine in the blend, such as ten-year-old, thirty-year-old and forty-year-old. 'Tawny' refers to the colour of the wine and the flavour is softer, more mature and slightly sweeter than Vintage Character or Late Bottled Vintage. As the wine has been kept in barrel all those years, it hasn't thrown a sediment in the bottle so doesn't need decanting.

Some traditionalists might turn in their graves, but it's great fun drinking these chilled. The producers do in the Douro, so why shouldn't we?

White Port makes an unusual aperitif, especially served with tonic. It's rather like Vermouth in flavour and an open bottle will keep quite some time in the fridge.

Good producers to look out for include Taylor, Dow, Warre, Fonseca, Graham and Quinta do Noval.

Madeira

A glass of Madeira m'dear? This expression makes it sound as if Madeira is a really old-wave drink, but if you're Winewise you'll give it a go, as it's a welcome alternative to sherry before the meal or instead of Port after the meal. It's made on the Portuguese island of Madeira, an idyllic place to go for a holiday. The islanders appear to risk death whilst harvesting the grapes, which are planted on steep terraced slopes which drop almost vertically into the sea. The vegetation is wonderfully mixed, and sugar cane can be found alongside the vines which are often trained up the trunks of banana trees.

Madeira is a fortified wine but made by a unique process where the grape must is heated. There are four basic types of Madeira, from dry to sweet, which take their name from the original vines used to make them. Sercial (often pale in colour) is the driest, made from a grape which is thought to be related to the Riesling. This is pleasant as an aperitif, with more body than Fino sherry, or served with strong gamey soup. Verdelho is a softer, slightly sweeter variety, but finishes with a dry tangy flavour. Bual is deeper in colour with a grapey, luscious flavour, and is nice to drink with fruit or nuts. Malmsey, the sweetest of them all, is excellent with pudding or in place of Port.

Some of the supermarkets are now selling their own-label Madeiras, which can be Winewise buys and really are excellent with food. Dinner guests will never know what to expect in a Winewise house, and it's experimenting with some of the more unusual wines that makes wine drinking so much fun.

Questionwise

This is designed as a quick reference guide for Winewise readers to answer some questions that might spring to mind. It's not designed to be comprehensive, so if you'd like fuller answers please refer to the relevant chapters.

Q. How many glasses of wine are there in a bottle, and how much do you order in a restaurant or if you are giving a party?

A. You can get six or seven glasses out of the average (75 cl) bottle. In a restaurant or for a party, generally allow for about half a bottle per head.

Q. Is it true that cheap plonk results in more of a hangover than expensive wine?

A. It depends how much you drink! But generally speaking, the better a wine the more you can drink without feeling lousy the following morning.

Q. Is mixing Champagne, white and red wine during a meal a bad idea?

A. No. But it isn't a good idea to mix spirits and wine or beer and wine – the old saying that grape and grain don't go together is, in my experience, very accurate.

Q. How do you get inside a bottle of Champagne or sparkling wine?

A. Grab the cork with one hand and the bottle with the other. Twist the bottle slowly round the cork and, when the cork is about to pop out, press on it so that the gas escapes slowly out of the narrow space left between the cork and the bottle. Don't shake the bottle about and spray it everywhere like a racing driver – that's just a waste of good fizz and flying corks can hurt people.

Q. Is decanting a wine really necessary?

A. That depends on the age of the wine. If it's an old wine, it's likely to have thrown a sediment. Whilst this is not harmful, it can detract from your pleasure in drinking the wine as the bits are rather unappetising. Decanting the bottle into a jug or decanter will leave the sediment in the bottle and a clear, bright wine in the decanter. To decant a bottle, open it carefully in an upright position. Then, preferably with a bright light shining underneath the bottle, tilt the bottle (label up) slowly until wine starts to pour out into the decanter. Continue pouring until you see the bits of sediment start to move towards the neck of the bottle. Once they've reached the neck, stop, leaving as little wine as possible (with the sediment in it) in the bottle. Decanting can also be used to aerate a wine. This can be very effective when you have a young red wine which is still tannic. The effect of aeration makes the wine seem to develop faster than it would otherwise, making it more pleasant to drink.

Q. How long can you keep a wine once the bottle has been opened?

A. It depends on the wine and how much there is left in the bottle. If you've got a proper bottle stopper it can keep easily for twenty-four hours, provided the bottle isn't almost empty and the wine has enough body. Light wines tend to go off more quickly than heavy ones, whites before reds. But some dessert and fortified wines can keep for up to two weeks once they're open. Wines always keep better if you leave them in the fridge.

Q. Should I send back a wine in a restaurant if there are crystals or sediment in the bottom of the bottle?

A. No. This is not a fault in the wine and will not affect the taste. You just have to be careful when pouring it.

Q. What is a fortified wine?

A. It's a wine to which alcohol has been added to increase the strength. Commonly found fortified wines include

Port, Muscat de Beaumes de Venise, Sherry and
Madeira.

Q. How can you tell how strong a wine is?

A. On most New World wines the strength is expressed on
the bottle as an alcohol percentage. The normal
strength for a table wine is between 11 per cent and 12
per cent, although many German wines can be as low
as 9 per cent. But if there's no indication on the label,
you can look at the 'legs' or 'tears' of the wine. Swirl it
round in the glass and let it settle. You will see lines of
liquid appearing on the insides of the glass which will
be more pronounced the stronger the wine.

Q. Are lead capsules dangerous?

A. Yes and no. If the capsule is not cut off at least half a
centimetre from the top of the bottle, there is a very
small risk that the wine coming into contact with the
capsule when poured will have trace elements of lead in
it. But quite honestly this is so insignificant as to be
almost negligible.

Q. Do dirty or torn labels mean the wine has been stored
badly?

A. If the wine is old, the labels will often be marked
because the bottles might well have been stored in a
damp cellar. This does not harm the wine at all.
However, sometimes you see a vertical streak of wine
running down the label. This is a very bad sign – it
means that the bottle has been kept standing up and in
a warm place so that some of the wine has been forced
out between the bottle and the cork and has dribbled
down the side. If you see a bottle like this you would be
well advised to send it back.

Q. What's an organic wine?

A. It's a wine from vineyards which are tended without the
use of artificial fertilisers or nutrients. Often special
weeds are grown between the rows of vines and are
then ploughed back in to provide fertilisation.

Q. Why do some wine waiters smell the cork once they
have taken it out of the bottle?

A. Because it is a widespread fallacy that you can tell if a
wine is corked by smelling the cork. This is not true,

and often the cork from a perfectly decent bottle will
smell rather fusty.

Q. If the cork crumbles when you open the bottle does it
mean that it's a bad wine?

A. No. If it crumbles and it is a young wine it means that
the producer has used cheap corks, but this won't
necessarily mean that the wine is bad. However, if the
wine is old, it is quite normal for the cork to crumble
and great care has to be taken in withdrawing it.

Q. Should the cork have the vintage stamped on it?

A. In practice no, but I would be happier if all corks had
the vintage on them. At the moment, only the top
producers stamp the vintage on the cork.

Q. If the wine is sold in a wooden case, does it mean that
it's good quality?

A. It can do. The top wines of Bordeaux, some of those
from Burgundy, some top Riojas, and Vintage Port all
come in wooden cases. But there are many other wines
which are available in wooden cases as presentation
packs and there is no guarantee that a wooden case will
mean top quality wine.

Q. Is it always cheaper to buy by the case?

A. It can be. Supermarkets don't generally give case
discounts, but most traditional wine merchants do. The
discount given is generally about 5 per cent.

Q. Does a wine always get better if it is opened a little
while before drinking?

A. No, virtually never. It is a fallacy that, by drawing the
cork and leaving the wine in the bottle, the wine
'breathes'. It can get rid of the sometimes musty smell
of the air between the cork and the wine, but the area
of wine in contact with the air is so small that it will
not aerate the wine at all. The only way to do this is by
decanting it.

Q. Do you have to use high-quality wine for cooking?

A. Many tests and tastings have been made to determine
this point. Often the answer appears to be that it
doesn't matter what type of wine you use for cooking,

provided the colour is right. However, my husband, who
is a wine merchant, often has access to a large number
of bottles after tastings. Some of these are of very good
quality indeed, and he believes that the better the wine
the better the sauce will be!

Q. What colour is Vinho Verde?

A. White.

Q. What wine is best used for a spritzer?

A. A spritzer is a mixture of white wine and soda or
sparkling mineral water, and it's a good way to drink
cheap white wine as a long drink without getting too
drunk. The best type of wine to use is light dry wine
like Muscadet.

Q. Is an older wine always better than a younger one?

A. Not necessarily. As each wine is different, so the length
of time that they can be kept varies. For example, a
Muscadet is unlikely to improve after two years'
ageing. A minor Bordeaux château is unlikely to keep
for more than about five or six years, whereas a great
Bordeaux château might keep for twenty, thirty years
or even longer.

Q. What's the difference between Trocken and
Trockenbeerenauslese on a German wine label?

A. Trocken is the driest German wine you can buy and
Trockenbeerenauslese is the sweetest! Yes, it is
confusing!

Q. What sort of wines go well with pudding?

A. The best combination is either a sweet or fortified wine,
or a Champagne or Cava.

Q. Are Pouilly Fuissé and Pouilly Fumé from the same
area?

A. No. Pouilly Fuissé is from Burgundy and Pouilly Fumé
is from the Loire, and they are made from different
grape varieties.

Wine Terms

The following are terms that are commonly used to describe
wines:

Corked	The wine has a definite smell and taste of mouldy corks.
Long	Maybe the length of your pocket if it's an expensive bottle, but generally used to describe a wine whose taste lingers on your taste buds for minutes after you've swallowed it or spat it out.
Drying out	Once a wine – normally red – reaches a specific age, it loses its fruit and is said to be 'drying out'. It's also how you might feel after a particularly heavy night on the booze.
Oxidised	When a wine is exposed to the air the oxygen reacts with the wine, making it taste unpleasant. This can also happen if a cork shrinks (because it has been kept standing up and the cork has not remained damp).
Bouquet/nose	Not a bunch of flowers that you hand to the wine waiter, but the smell of a wine.
Carafe wine/jug wine	Cheap quaffing wine, often from America.

Index

Adgestone vineyard, 150
Adnams wines, 79–80
alcoholic strength, 28–9, 180
Almeirim wine cooperative, 143
Aloxe-Corton, 115
Alsace wines, 34, 35, 42, 83–4, 138–40; bottle, 19; Grands Crus, 140; labels, 138
l'Alsacien (company), 83–4, 140
'Les Amis du Vin' wine club, 96
Amontillado Sherry, 35, 174
l'Angélus, 126
Appellation Contrôlée (AC), 21, 24, 28, 158
Armagnac, 77
l'Arrosée, 126
Asda, 76–7
Asti Spumante, 43. 153
auctions, 85–8; 'buyer's premium', 87; 'duty paid' or 'in bond' wines, 87
Auslese wines, 157, 158
Australian wines, 18, 19, 35, 41, 42, 43, 46, 75, 77, 82, 161–5; bag-in-box wines, 21–2, 164; liqueur Muscats, 19, 35, 163–4; red, 164; white, 162–3
Auxey-Duresses, 91, 114, 115

bag-in-box wines, 21–2, 76, 164, 172
Bahans-Haut-Brion, 125
Bairrada, 35, 142
Baker, Bill, 82
Bandol, 135
Barbadillo, 174
Barbaresco, 36, 46, 153
Barbera, 36, 153
Bardolino, 153

Barolo, 36, 38, 46, 58, 66, 153
Barossa Valley wines, 161, 163
Barsac, 35, 120, 122, 127
Barton Manor vineyard, 150
Beaujolais, 18, 36, 69, 113, 117–19; Crus, 35; Grands Crus, 118–19
Beaujolais Nouveau, 44, 117–18, 167
Beaujolais Villages, 118
Beaumes de Venise, 134
Beaune, 114, 115
Beerenauslese, 31, 157
Belfrage, Nick, 79, 152
Belin, 114
Bellevue-Mondotte, 126
Bergerac, 17, 35, 75, 128–9
Berri Estates, 165
Berry, Liz and Mike, 83
Beyer, 140
Bianco di Custoza, 153
Bibendum wine tastings, 95
Biddenden vineyard, 150
'Billy Whizz', 80–1
Bischöfliche Priesterseminar, 159
Bize, 115
Blagn-Gagnard, 115
Blanquette de Limoux, 19
blush wines, 46, 171
bockbeutel, 19
Bodegas Roijanas, 145
Bollinger Champagne, 101
Bon Gran, 116
Le Bon-Pasteur, 126
Bordeaux, 34, 35, 36, 38, 41, 45, 58, 66, 77, 78, 79, 80, 82, 83, 112, 117, 120–7, 144, 181, 182; bottle shape, 17, 121; Châteaux second wines, 125; en primeur, 80–1, 124; Médoc, 124–5; Petits Châteaux wines, 122–3, 182; Pomerol, 126; Saint-Emilion, 125–6; sweet, 120, 127; vintages, 121; white, 120, 122, 126–7
Bordeaux Sauvignon, 126
Bordeaux Supérieur, 121, 123

Bortoli, de, 165
bottles, 17–21; Alsace, 19; Bordeaux, 17; Burgundy, 17–18; Champagne, 19; corks and corkscrews, 54–9; German, 18–19; number of glasses in, 178; opening champagne, 105–6, 178–9; plastic, 20; sizes, 19–21
Bouchard Père et Fils, 112
Bourgogne Aligoté, 114
Bourgogne Blanc, 113, 114, 115
Bourgogne Rouge, 113, 114
Bourgueil, 36, 45, 110
brandy balloons, 63
Breaky Bottom vineyard, 150
British Home Stores, 74
British Sherry, 173–4
British wine, 148; *see also* English wine
Brouilly, 119
Brown Brothers, 165
Brunello di Montepulciano, 36, 154
Bual (Madeira), 35, 177
Bulgarian wines, 35, 41, 45, 160
Bull's Blood, 36
Burgundy, 38, 44, 80, 82, 83, 111–16, 181; bottle shape, 17–18; Chablis, 113–14; Côte Chalonnaise, 115; Côte de Beaune, 114–15; Côte de Nuits, 114; *en primeur*, 79; Mâconnais, 115–16; negociants and growers, 112; vintages, 30; white, 34, 41, 114–16
Bürklin-Wolf, 159
Butler's Friend, 57
Buzet, 17, 35, 75, 129–30

Cabernet Franc, 45, 110, 120, 128, 129, 146, 153
Cabernet Sauvignon, 44, 45, 120, 128, 129, 135, 137, 143, 146, 154; Australian, 164; Bulgarian, 35, 45, 160; Californian, 45, 170–1; Chilean, 35, 67, 172; Hungarian, 45; New Zealand, 167
Cadet Piola, 126
Cahors, 17, 130
Cairanne, 133
Californian wines, 18, 36, 40, 41, 42, 44, 45, 46, 82, 168–71; 'blush' wines, 46, 171; boutique wineries, 169; carafe/jug wines, 169, 183
Canon Fronsac, 122
Cap de Mourlin, 126

carafe/jug wines, 169, 183
Carmignano, 154
Carr-Taylor vineyard, 150
Cassis, 135
Cava, 19, 47, 182
Cave Coop, 116
Cavendish Manor vineyard, 150
Cérons, 127
Certan de May, 126
Chablis, 33, 35, 90, 109, 113–14
La Chablisienne, 114
Chalone, 171
Champagne, 15, 33, 44, 58, 75, 76, 77, 100–6, 182; Blanc de Blancs, 41, 104; Blanc des Noirs, 37, 44; bottle, 19; 'Deluxe', 104; glasses, 60-1; non-vintage, 32, 103; opening bottles, 105–6, 178–9; Rosé, 104; vintage, 32, 103
Champagne Jacquesson, 84
champagne pincers, 58
Champalimaud, Miguel, 141
Chandon de Briailles, 115
Chanté Cigal, 134
Chardonnay, 18, 34, 38, 39, 101, 104, 111, 113, 115, 116, 143, 146, 152, 153; Australian, 41, 162–3; Bulgarian, 41, 160; Californian, 41, 169–70; Chilean, 172; New Zealand, 41, 166
Chassagne, 34, 114
Chassagne-Montrachet, 115
Chasse-Spleen, 125
Château Brane Cantenac, 125
Château de Clairefont, 125
Château de la Jaubertie, 128–9
Château d'Issan, 124
Château Ducru Beaucaillou, 125
Château Grand-Puy-Lacoste, 125
Château-Grillet, 133
Château Gruaud-Larose, 125
Château Haut-Bages-Libéral, 124
Château Haut-Bailly, 125
Château Haut-Batailley, 124
Château Haut-Brion, 125
Château Kirwan, 124
Château Lafite-Rothschild, 55–6
Château La Lagune, 133
Château Langoa-Barton, 124
Château Léoville-Barton, 124
Château Léoville Lascases, 125
Château Margaux, 125

Château Montrose, 15, 125
Châteauneuf-du-Pape, 35, 36, 133–4
Château Pichon-Longuéville-Lalande, 125
Château Prieuré-Lichine, 125
Château Rayas, 134
Château St Jean, 171
Château St Pierre, 124
Château Talbot, 125
Château Val Joanis, 136
Château Vignelaure, 135
Chave, 133
Chénas, 119
Chenin Blanc, 107, 109; Californian, 170; New Zealand, 167
Chianti, 35, 90, 151, 154
Chilean wines, 36, 67, 172
chilling wine, 67–9, 71
Chinon, 36, 45, 110
Chiroubles, 118
Christie's auction house, 85, 86, 87–8
Cinsault (grape), 137
Cissac, 125
Clair-Dau, 115
Clape, 133
Claret *see* Bordeaux
Clerc, 115
Clerget, 114, 115
Clos du Marquis, 125
Clos du Val, 171
Codorniu, 147
Cognac, 44
Cogny, 115
Colliers, Bigwood and Bewlay, auction house, 88
Concha y Toro, 172
Condrieu, 133
Connétable de Talbot, 125
cooking wine, 181–2
Cook's wines, 167
Coonawarra wines, 161
Corbières, 17, 36
'The Cork and Bottle', wine bar, 96
corks and corkscrews, 54–9, 180–1
Cornas, 36, 46, 132
Corton, 115
Côte Chalonnaise, 113, 115
Côte de Beaune, 113, 114–15
Côte de Beaune-Villages, 115
Côte de Bergerac AC, 129
Côte de Brouilly, 119
Côte de Nuits, 113, 114

Côte de Nuits Villages, 114
Côte d'Or, 35, 113, 115
Côte d'Or Burgundy, 36
Côte Mâconnais, 113
Côte Rôtie, 36, 46, 132
Coteaux d'Aix-en-Provence, 133
Coteaux des Baux-en-Provence, 136
Coteaux du Layon, 35
Coteaux du Tricastin, 46, 133
Côtes de Bourg et Blaye, 122, 126
Côtes de Castillon, 122
Côtes de Duras, 130
Côtes de Francs, 36, 122, 126
Côtes de Mermandais, 131
Côtes de Provence, 135
Côtes du Luberon, 136
Côtes-du-Rhône, 19, 36, 46, 89, 132, 133
Côtes-du-Rhône-Villages, 133
Côtes du Ventoux, 36, 46, 133
Côtes du Vivarais, 133
Cousiño Macul, 172
'The Crown', Southwold, 79–80
Crozes-Hermitage, 36, 46, 132
Cuvée Napoléon, 129–30
CVNE, Bodega, 145

La Dame de Montrose, 125
Dão wines, 36, 142
Davis winemaking College, University of California, 168, 169
Davisons wine shops, 79
Davy's wine bars, 96
Decanter magazine, 95
decanting wine, 65–7, 179, 181; Vintage Port, 175–6
Deinhard, 159
diethylene glycol (DEG) scandal, 158
DOC (Italian Denominazione di Origine Controllata), 24, 26, 151
DOCG, Italian, 26, 151
Dolcetto, 153
Dom Hermano wines, 143
Domaine Benoît, 127
Domaine de Beaucastel, 134
Domaine de Chevalier, 127
Domaine de Fieuzal, 127
Domaine de Fontarney/Ch Notton, 125
Domaine de Jarras, 137
Domaine de la Renarde, 115
Domaine de la Romanée Conti, 114

Domaine des Arnevels, 134
Domaine de Trevallon, 136
Domaine Direct, 80
Domaine Viticole des Salins du Midi, 137
Domecq, 174
Douro wines, 141–2, 175
Dow, 177
Dreyer, Sick, 140
Drouhin, Joseph, 112
Drouhin-Larose, 114
Duboeuf, 116
Dubreuil-Fontaine, 115
Dujac, 114
Durup, 114

Edna Valley, 171
l'Eglise-Clinet, 126
Eiswein, 158
Emilia Romagnia wines, 154
English wine, 148–50
Entre-Deux-Mers, 33, 34, 41, 120, 121, 122, 123, 126
Esmeralda, 146
'The Epworth Tap', 96
EVA (English Vineyards Association), 150

Farr Vintners, 80
fermentation, 38, 102
Fèvre, 114
Findlater, Alex, wine-tastings, 95
Fitou, 17, 36, 75
Fixin, 114
Fleurie, 119
Fombrauge, 126
Fonroque, 126
Fonseca, J.M. da, 143, 177
food and wines, 93–4
fortified wines, 29, 161, 173–7, 179–80, 182; Australian liqueur Muscats, 19, 35, 163–4; Madeira, 177; Muscat de Beaumes de Venise, 29, 42, 134; Port, 174–7; Sherry, 173–4
Franc Grâce Dieu, 126
Frascati, 19, 34, 44, 151
Freixenet, 147
French wines, 100–40; alcoholic strength, 28–9; Alsace, 138–40; Beaujolais, 117–19; Bordeaux, 120–7; Burgundy, 111–16;

Champagne, 100–6; classifications, 24; labels, 25; Loire, 107–10; Provençal, 135–7; Rhône Valley, 132–4; South-West France, 128–31
Friedrich Wilhelm Gymnasium, 159
Friuli wines, 153–4
Fronsac, 36, 122, 126
Fumé Blanc *see* Sauvignon Blanc

Gaillac, 130–1
Gallo wines, 169
Gamay, 44, 110, 117; Calfornian, 44
Garnacha, 46, 144
Garrafeira wine, 141, 142
German wines, 35, 36, 43, 156–9; bottles, 18–19; classifications and labels, 24, 25–6, 157–8; Riesling, 42, 158; sweet wines, 157–8; vintages, 157–8
Gevrey-Chambertin, 111
Gewürztraminer, 43, 138–9, 146, 152, 166
Gibbs, Hilary, 80
Gigondas, 133
Girard-Vollot, 115
Gisborne wines, 167
Gisselbrecht, 140
Givry, 115
Gore-Brown Trophy, 150
Graham, 177
Grande Escolha, 142
grapes, varieties of, 40–7
Gras, 115
Graves, 35, 41, 43, 120, 121, 122, 126–7
Grenache (Garnacha), 46, 135, 137, 144, 164
Gris de Gris, 137
Gros, Jean, 115
Gros Plant, 34, 108–9
Guigal, 133

Hardy, 164
Haut-Médoc, 121
Hawkes Bay wines, 167
Heidsieck Monopole, 103
Heitz, 171
Hermitage, 36, 46, 132
Hewitson, Don, 96
high-street chains, 77–9
Hill Smith, 165
Hilliards, 77

Houghton Supreme, 165
Howard Ripley Wines, 82–3
Hugel, 140
Hungarian wines, 45
Hungerford Wine Company, 80–1
Hunter Valley wines, 161, 163
Huxelrebe (grape), 43

International Wine Auctions, 88
Iron Horse, 171
Italian wine, 44, 46, 75, 79, 151–5;
    classifications and labels, 24, 26–7

Jaboulet Aîné, Paul, 133
Jadot, Louis, 112
Jasmin, 133
Jayer, 114
Jordan, 171
Juliénas, 119
Jurançon, 131

Kabinett, 157
Khan Krum Reserve Chardonnay,
    160
Kreydenweiss, Marc, 140
Krug Champagne, 103, 104; Grand
    Cuvée, 104

labels, 23–9, 180
Lacoste-Boire, 125
La Croix, 125
Lacy Scott auction house, 88
Lafleur, 126
Lafon, 115
Lalande de Pomerol, 126
La Mancha wines, 146
Lamberhurst, 150
Lamblin, 114
Lambrusco, 19, 36, 151, 154; white,
    33
Landwein, German, 24
Larmande, 126
Lasserat, 126
Latium wines, 155
Latour, Louis, 112
Lay and Wheeler, 81–2; annual wine
    workshops, 82
Laflaive, 115
Léon, Jean, 146
Lello Reserva, 142
Leroy, 114
Liebfraumilch, 33, 35, 156, 157, 159

Lindeman, 165
Linderos, 172
Liqueur Muscat, Australian, 19, 35,
    163–4
Lirac, 36
Listel, 137
Loftus, Simon, 79
Loire wines, 84, 107–10
Long-Depaquit, 114
Loron, 116
Loupiac, 120, 122, 127
La Louvière, 127
Lucquet, 116
Lussac, 126
Lustau, 174
Luxembourg wines, 34

macération carbonique, 38–9, 117,
    131
Mâcon, 34, 116
Mâcon-Clessé, 116
Mâcon-Fuissé, 116
Mâcon-Loché, 116
Mâcon-Luguy, 116
Mâcon-Prissé, 116
Mâcon-Rouge, 116
Mâcon-Villages, 116
Mâcon-Vinzelles, 116
Mâcon-Viré, 116
Mâconnais, 115–16
Madelaine-Angevine (grape), 43
Madeira wine, 29, 177, 180; Bual, 35,
    177; Malmsey, 35, 177; Sercial, 35,
    177; Verdelho, 177
Madiran, 36, 131
Majestic Wine Warehouses, 84
Malartic-Lagravière, 127
Malbec (grape), 120, 153
Malmsey (Madeira), 35, 177
Manzanilla, 174
Marchard de Gramant, 115
Margaux, 121
Mark West Vineyards, 171
The Market (chain wine shops), 79,
    152
Marks and Spencer's, 76
Marlborough wines, 167
Marqués de Caceres, Bodega, 145
Marqués de Riscal, Bodega, 145
Marsala, 155
Masson, Paul, 171
Mateus Rosé, 19, 128, 141
Matrot, 115

maturing of wines, 38–9
Médoc, 120, 121, 126; Crus Bourgeois, 124–5; Grand Cru Classé, 124
Mehana, 160
Mendocino wines, 169
Ménétou-Salon, 34, 41, 90, 110
merchants' wine-tastings, 83, 95
Mercurey, 115
Merlot, 45–6, 120, 128, 129, 153, 154, 160, 170
Merril, Geoff, 164–5
Mersault, 34, 90, 113, 115
Methanol scandal (Italy, 1986), 151
méthode champenoise, 101. 109, 147
'Methuselah's', wine bar, 96
Meyney, 125
Michel, Bernard, 115
Michel, Louis, 114
Michelot, 114, 115
Millot-Battault, 115
Minervois, 17
Monbazillac, 35, 120, 122, 131
Monbrison, 125
Mondavi, 171
Mont Redon, 134
Montague St Emilion, 122
Montaguy, 115
Montalivet, 127
Montana, 167
Montepulciano *see* Brunello; Vino Nobile
Morey, A., 115
Morey, P., 115
Morgon, 119
Morrisons, 77
Moscatel de Setúbal, 35
Moscato d'Asti, 43, 153
Mosel wine bottle, 18
Moulin-à-Vent, 119
Muga, Bodega, 145
Müller, 159
Müller-Thurgau, 43, 149, 158, 166
Murray River Valley wines, 161
Muscadet, 33, 34, 107, 110, 117, 182; grape (Melon de Bourgogne), 41, 43; de Sèvre-et-Maine, 107; -sur-Lie, 107
Muscat, 42–3, 139, 146, 152, 160; Australian liqueur, 19, 35, 42, 163–4
Muscat de Beaumes de Venise, 29, 33, 35, 42, 134, 180
Muscat de Rivesaltes, 42

Napa Valley wines, 169, 170
Navarra, 36, 145–6
Nebbiolo (grape), 46
New Hall vineyard, 150
New York State wines, 82
New Zealand wines, 34, 36, 41, 42, 166–7
'Le Nez Rouge', wine club, 96
Niellon, 115
Nuits St Georges, 111, 114

Oddbins, 77–8
off-licence chains, 78
Olarra, Bodega, 145
Oregon wines, 82
organic wine, 180
Orlando, 165
Ormes-de-Pez, 125
Orvieto, 35
Ostlers (wine shop), 82; wine tastings, 95
oxidisation, 183

Palette, 135
La Parde de Haut-Bailly, 125
Pauillac, 121, 124
Pavie-Decesse, 126
Pavillon Rouge de Château Margaux, 125
Peatling and Cawdron (chain shops), 78–9
Pécharmant, 129
Penedés wines, 45, 146–7
Penfold's, 165, 167
Pernand-Vergelesses, 114, 115
Peter Dominic, 78
Petit Verdot (grape), 120
Petrus, 126
Phelps, Joseph, 171
Philips, Son and Neil, auction house, 88
Phylloxera (vine-eating louse), 44, 144, 166
Pic, 114
pichet bottles, 19
Piedmontese wines, 153
Pinot Blanc (Bianco), 139, 152, 153
Pinot Gris or Tokay, 139
Pinot Meunier, 101
Pinot Noir, 18, 44–5, 101, 104, 111, 113, 115, 139–40, 164; Californian, 170; New Zealand, 167

Pinotage (grape), 167
Piper Heidsieck Champagne, 103
Piramimma, 165
Pires, João, 143; Dry Moscato, 143
Pol Roger Champagne, 103
Pomerol, 36, 45, 120, 121, 126
Pommard, 114
Port, 27, 29, 36, 42, 141, 174–7, 180;
    Late Bottled Vintage, 176; Tawny,
    176; Vintage, 32, 142, 175–6, 181;
    Vintage Character, 176; White,
    176–7
Portuguese wines, 19, 76, 77, 78, 128,
    141–3; labels, 27–8; Port, 174–7;
    red, 74–5, 141–3; white, 142, 143
Potensac, 125
Pouilly-Fumé, 34, 41, 109, 110, 182
Pouilly-Fuissé, 115, 116, 182
Pouilly-Vinzelles, 115, 116
Poujeaux, 125
Provençal wines, 84, 135–7
Prüm, J.J., 159
Puligny-Montrachet, 115
pupitre (rack), 102

Qualitätswein, German, 24
QbA and QmP wines, German, 26,
    157
Quincy, 34, 41, 90, 110
Quinta do Cotto, 141, 142
Quinta do Noval, 177

Rahoul, 127
Rasteau, 133
Raveneau, 114
Reciotto della Valpolicella Amarone,
    153
red wines: chilled, 69; heavy- to full-
    bodied, 36; light-bodied, 36;
    medium-bodied, 35; serving
    temperature, 69–70, 92; styles of,
    34; sweet, 36; varieties of grape,
    44–6; vinification process, 37, 38–9
Regaleali, 36, 75, 155
Reichensteiner (grape), 149
Reid, Charles, 82
Reid Wines, 82
Remoissenet Père et Fils, 112
Réserve de la Comtesse, 125
La Réserve wine tastings, 95
restaurants: bringing your own wine
    to, 96; ordering wine in, 89–92

Reuilly, 90, 110
Reynon, 127
Rhine Riesling, Californian, 42
Rhine wine bottle, 18
Rhône Valley wines, 35, 36, 79, 84,
    111, 132–4
Ridge Vineyards, 171
Riesling, 42, 138, 152, 158, 160;
    Alsace, 42, 139; Australian, 42,
    163; Bulgarian, 160; Californian
    (Johannisberg), 42, 170; German,
    42, 158; New World, 35; New
    Zealand, 166; Yugoslav, 19, 35, 42
Rioja, 17, 35, 36, 38, 45, 46, 144, 145,
    181; classifications, 145; new-style,
    144, 145; white, 145
Rioja Alta, Bodega, 145
Rion, 114
Ripley, Howard, 83
Roederere Champagne, 103
room temperature, 69, 92
rosé wines, 24, 37, 128, 130–1;
    Champagne, 104; de Provence, 135,
    136, 137; Portuguese, 19, 128, 141
Rosemount, 163, 165; Show Reserve,
    163
Rothbury, 165
Roty, 114
Roumier, 115
Rousseau, 114
Roussillon, 36
Rully, 115
Rutherford Hill, 171
Ryman, Henry, 128–9

Sainsbury's, 33, 74–5, 141, 151,
    153–4
St Amour, 118
St Aubin, 114, 115
St Emilion, 36, 45, 120, 121, 122,
    125–6
St Estèphe, 121
St Georges St Emilion, 122, 126
St Joseph, 36, 46, 132
St Julien, 121, 124
St Péray, 133
St Romain, 114, 115
St Véran, 115, 116
Sainte Croix-du-Mont, 122, 127
Sakar Mountain Cabernet, 160
Sancerre, 34, 36, 41, 44, 90, 109, 110
Santa Digna wines, 172
Santenay, 115

Sarget de Gruaud-Larose, 125
Saumur, 19, 109
Saumur-Champigny, 36, 110
Sauternes, 33, 35, 43, 93, 120, 122, 127
Sauvignon Blanc (Fumé Blanc), 18, 41–2, 109, 110, 126, 129, 130, 153, 154, 155, 163, 167; Australian, 163; Californian, 42, 170; Chilean, 172; New Zealand, 42, 167
Sauvignon de St Bris, 113–14
Sauvignon de Touraine, 34
Sauzet, 115
Savacentres, 74
Savigny-les-Beaune, 114, 115
Schloss Reinhartshausen, 159
Schramsberg, 170, 171
Schubert, 159
Schuster, Michael, 95
Screwpull, 56–7
Sekt, sparkling wine, 157
Sélection de Grains Nobles wine, 139
Semillon, 41, 43, 126, 129; Australian, 163; Chilean, 172
Sercial (Madeira), 34, 177
Servin, 114
Setúbal wines, 143
'Shampers', wine bar, 96
Sheppard, Ross, 82
Sherry, 29, 173–4, 180; Almacenista, 174; Amontillado, 35, 174; British, 173–4; Cream, 35, 174; Cyprus, 173; Fino, 34, 174; Oloroso, 174; South African, 173
Shiraz *see* Syrah
shopping for wine, 74–84; high street chains, 77–9; independents, 79–84; supermarkets, 33–4, 74–7
Sicilian wines, 75, 155
Smith-Haut-Lafitte, 127
Soave, 34, 151, 152
Sociando-Mallet, 125
Sonoma wines, 169
Sotheby's wine auctions, 85, 88
South-West France, wines of, 128–31
Spanish wines, 34, 75, 76, 77, 78, 144–7; labels, 27, 145; Sherry, 29, 34, 173–4
sparkling wines, 34, 124, 130; Asti Spumante, 43, 153; Cava, 147; Champagne, 100–6; Lambrusco, 33, 36, 151, 154; Moscato d'Asti,

153; St Péray, 133; Saumur, 109; Sekt, 157; Vouvray, 109
Spätlese wines, 35, 157, 158
'spiral cellar', 72
Spots Farm vineyard, 150
spritzer, 182
Stag's Leap, 171
supermarkets, 74–7, 101, 104, 122, 150, 151, 164, 177; wine-coding systems, 33–4
Swiss wines, 34
Sylvaner, 138, 139
Syrah (Shiraz) grape, 46, 135, 164

table wines, 23–4
Tafelwein, EEC, 23
Taltarni, 165
Taylor, 177
Taylor-Gill, Simon, 80
temperature of wine when served, 69–70, 92
Tempranillo (grape), 144
Tesco, 76, 151
tetrapacks or tetrabrics, 20–1, 54, 76
Three Choirs vineyard, 150
Tignanello, 91, 154
tins (cans) of wine, 20, 54
Tocai Friulano, 154
Tokay Aszu, 35
Tollot-Beaut, 115
Torres, Miguel, 45, 146, 172
Torres Black Label, 146
Torres Gran Vina Sol, 146
La Tour de By, 125
Tour de Haut Moulin, 125
La Tour-Martillac, 127
Touraine wines, 110
Traminer, 152
Trapet, 114
Trebbiano (grape), 43–4, 152
Trefethen Vineyards, 171
Trentino wines, 152
Trimbach, 140
Trocken, 34, 157, 158, 182
Trockenbeerenauslese, 35, 157–8, 182
Trotanoy, 126
Tuscany wines, 154
Tyrrell, 165

Ugni-Blanc (grape), 41, 43

Vacqueyras, 133
Valdepeñas, 146
Valdespino, 174
Valpolicella, 36, 151, 152, 153
'varietal' wines, 40, 171
VDQS (Vins Délimités de Qualité
    Supérieure), 24, 108, 131, 136
Vendange Tardive wines, 139
Veneto wines, 152–3
Verdelho (Madeira), 177
Veuve-Clicquot Champagne, 101, 103
Victoria wines, 161, 163
Victoria Wine shops, 78
Vienot, Charles, 112
Vieux-Château-Certan, 126
Vieux Télégraph, 134
La Vigneronne, 83; wine-tastings, 83,
    95
Villaine, 115
Vin de Pay, French, 24, 34, 36, 110,
    128, 130, 136, 137
Vin de Pays des Sables du Golfe du
    Lion, 137
Vincent, 116
Vinho Verde, 19, 182
'Vinicool', 69
vinification, 37–9
Vino da Tavola, Italian, 26
Vino Nobile di Montepulciano, 154
vintage(s), 30–2; Champagne, 32,
    103; Port, 32, 142, 175–6
Viura (grape), 145
Volnay, 114
Von Buhl, 159
Vouvray, 35, 109; Moelleux, 35, 109;
    Sparkling, 109

Waiter's Friend, 57
Waitrose, 75–6, 151
Warre, 177

Westbury vineyard, 150
Which? Wine Guide, 96
white wines: chilling, 67–9; dry, full-
    bodied, 34–5; dry, light to medium-
    bodied, 34; grape varieties, 41–4;
    medium-sweet, light-to-medium-
    bodied, 35; *perlé*, 130; serving too
    cold, 92; style coding systems, 33–
    4; vinification process, 37–8; *see
    also* sparkling wines
Wine magazine, 95
Wine and Spirit Education Trust
    courses, 96
wine bars, 96
wine cellars, 71, 72–3
wine classifications, 23–4
wine clubs, 96
wine coding systems, 33–4
wine decanters, 65, 67
Wine Development Board, 95
wine fridges, 71–2
wine glasses, 60–4
wine lists, 89–91
wine racks, 71
The Wine Society, 96
wine styles, 33–6; codes, 33; reds, 35–
    6; whites, 34–5
wine-tasting, 48–50, 82, 83, 85, 95–6;
    blind, 52, 75; clubs, 95; merchants',
    83, 95
wine terms, 24–8, 50–1, 145, 182–3
Winewise wine tastings, 95
wooden cases of wine, 181
Wootton vineyard, 150
Wynns, 165

Yalumba, 165
Yapp Brothers, 84, 136
Yugoslav Riesling, 42; Laski, 19, 35

Zinfandel, 36, 46, 170–1